BOOK • VIDEO

HOT LICKS

ERIC JOHNSON

TOTAL ELECTRIC GUITAR

I0792509

To access video visit:
www.halleonard.com/mylibrary

Enter Code
2839-6374-9723-4587

ISBN 978-1-4950-8712-7

Music Sales America

HAL•LEONARD®

7777 W. BLUEMOUND RD. P.O. BOX 13819 MILWAUKEE, WI 53213

CONTENTS

Chapter 1: Picking Techniques

Example 1: Bounce Techniques
(1:41)

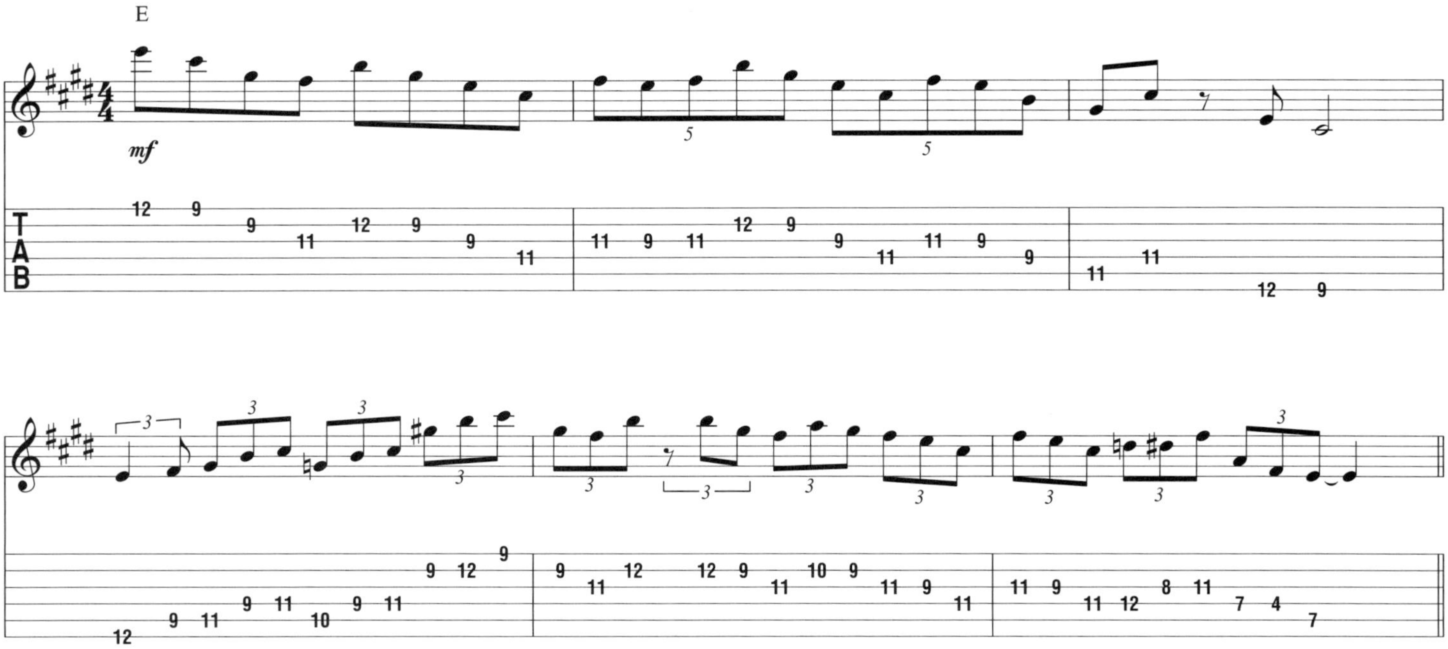

Example 2
(1:51)

Example 3
(2:18)

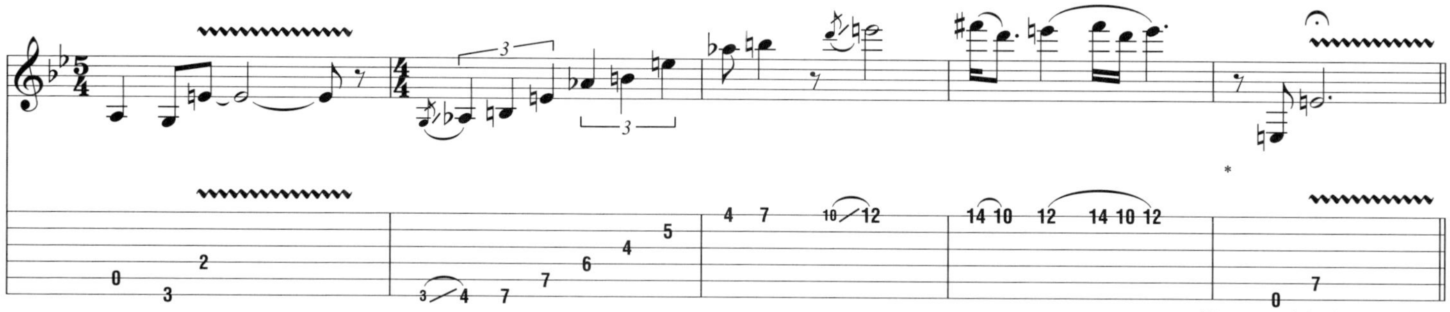

*Decrease vol. knob to 1/2 volume.

Example 4
(3:17)

*Downstroke
**Upstroke

Example 5
(3:36)

Example 6
(4:30)

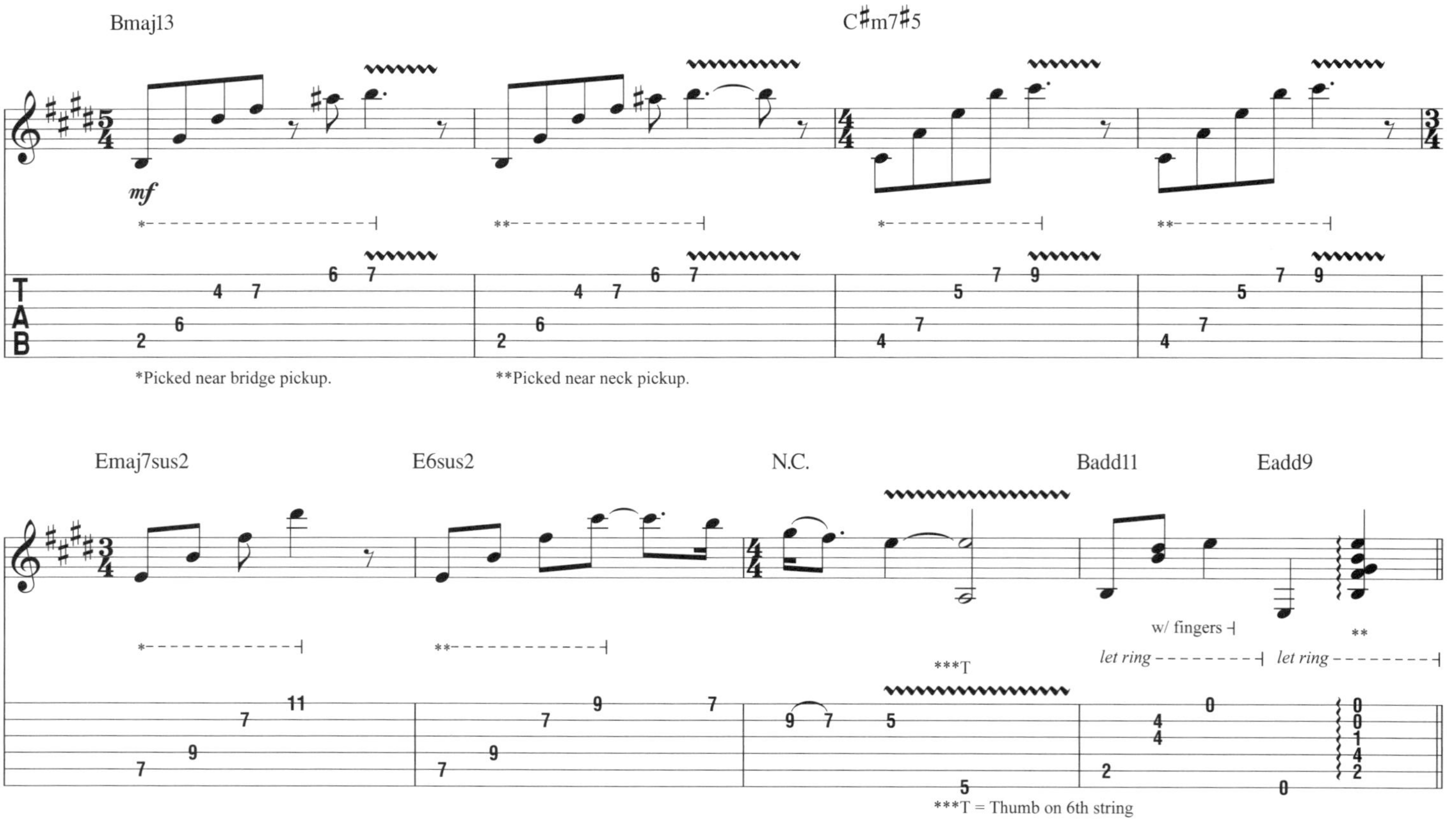

Example 7 (Fig. 1 on video)
(5:17)

Example 8 (Fig. 2 on video)
(5:25)

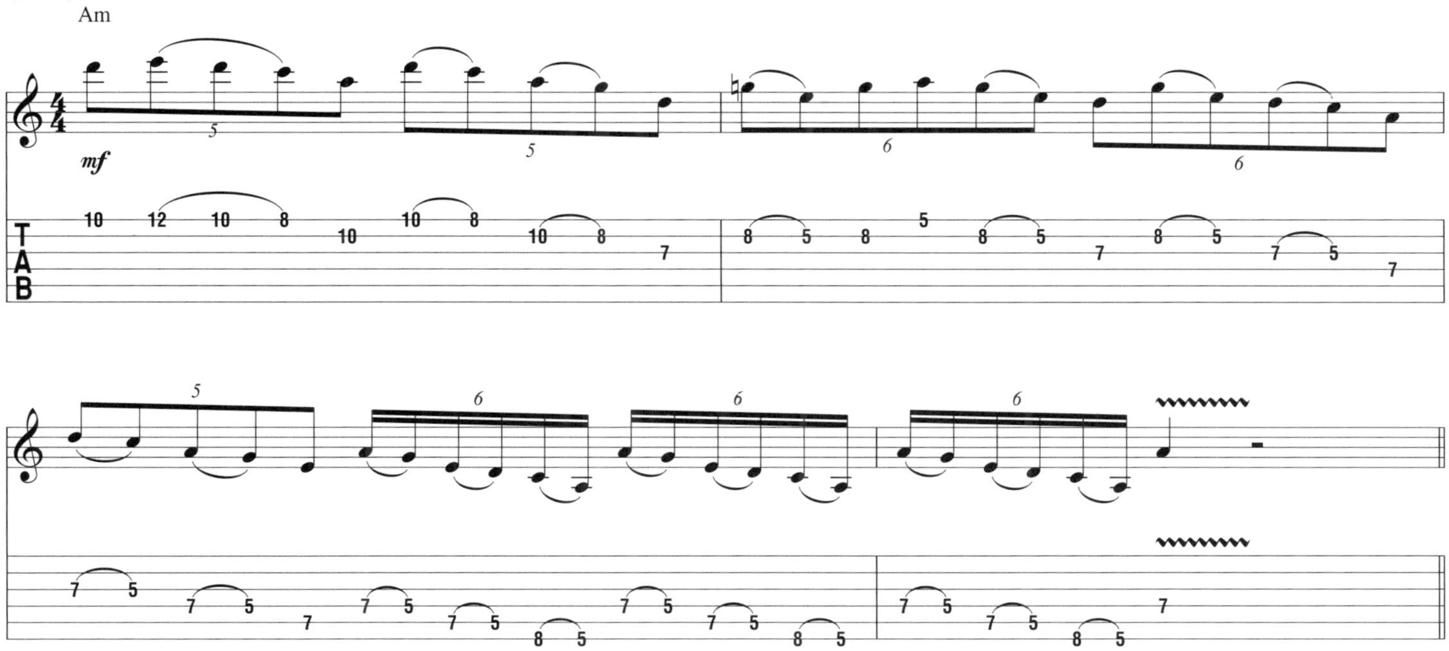

Example 9
(5:37)

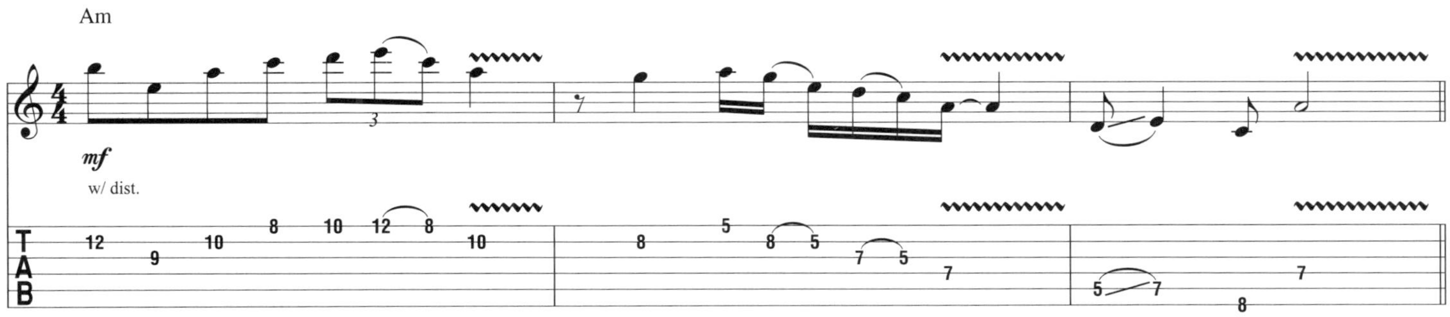

Example 10
(5:45)

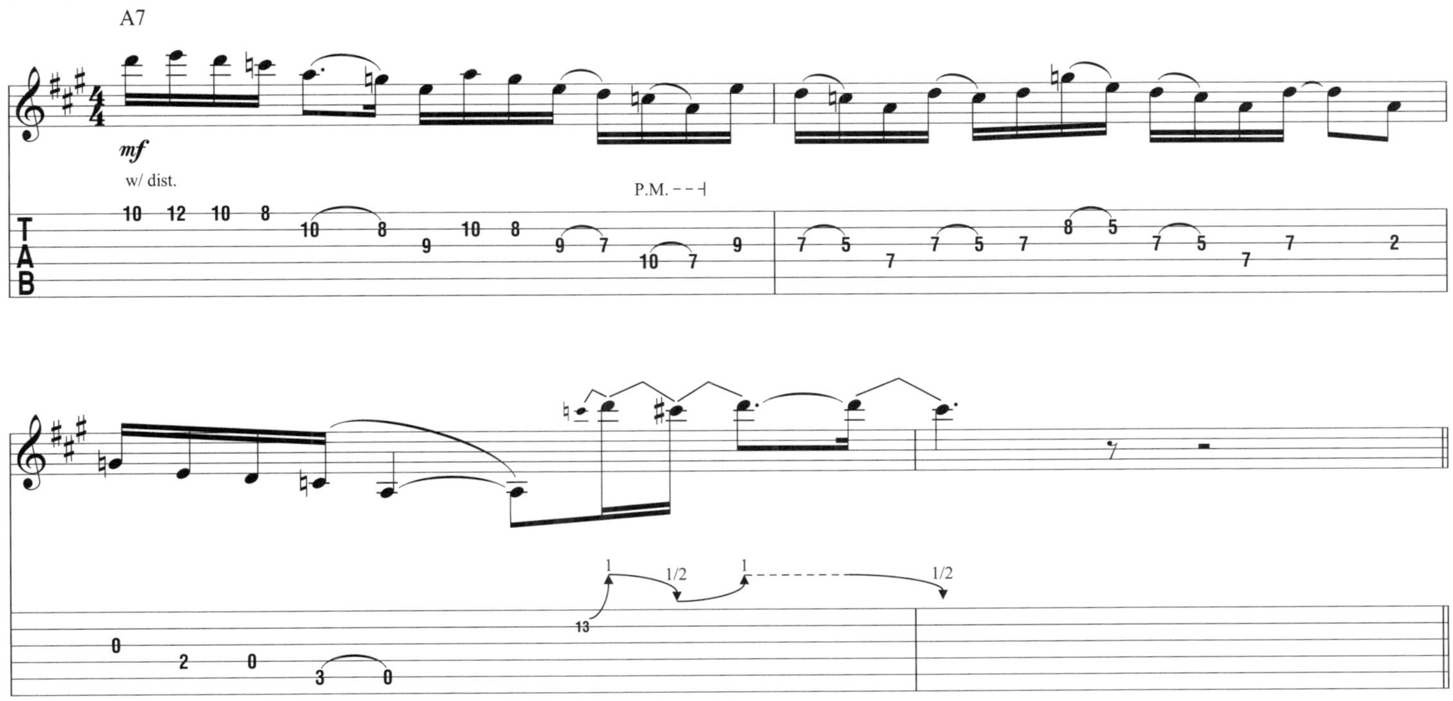

Example 11 (Fig. 3 on video)
(6:24)

Example 12
(7:45)

Example 13 (Fig. 4 on video)
(8:07)

Example 14 (Fig. 5 on video)
(8:21)

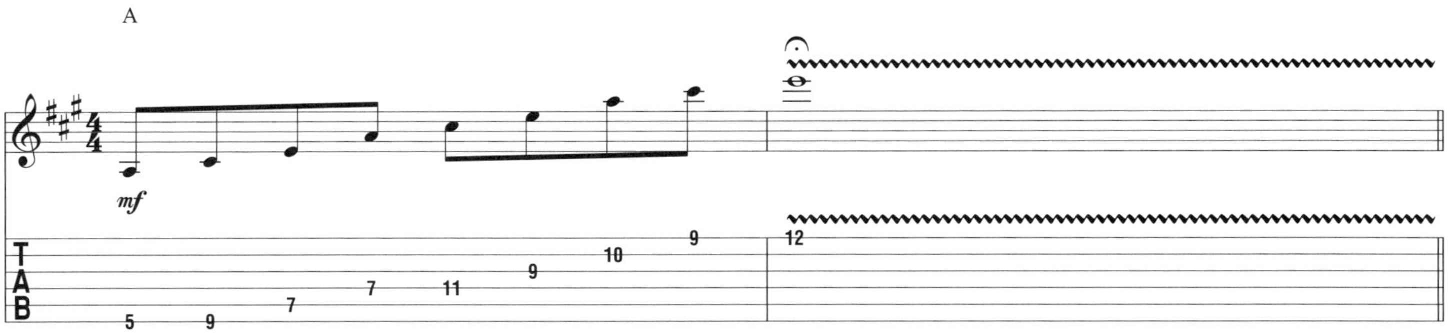

Example 15 (Fig. 6 on video)
(8:24)

Example 16 (Fig. 7 on video)
(8:32)

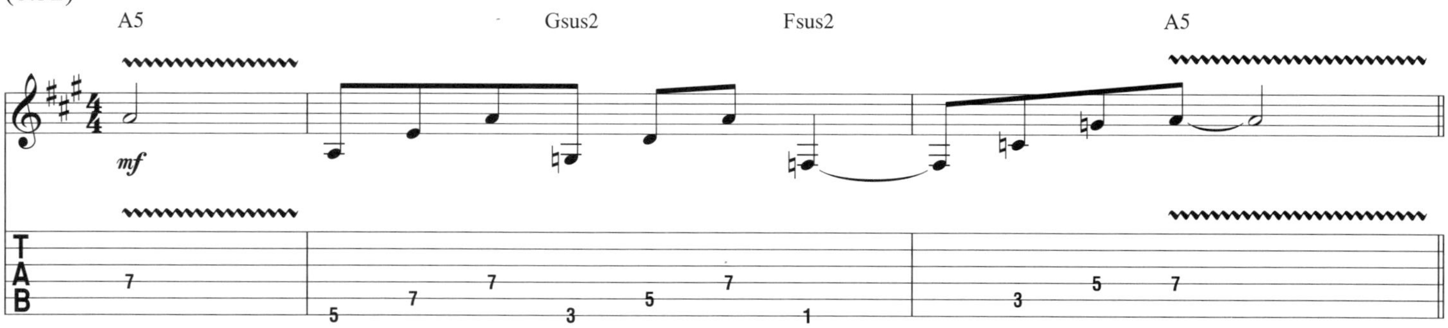

Example 17: Piano style
(0:13)

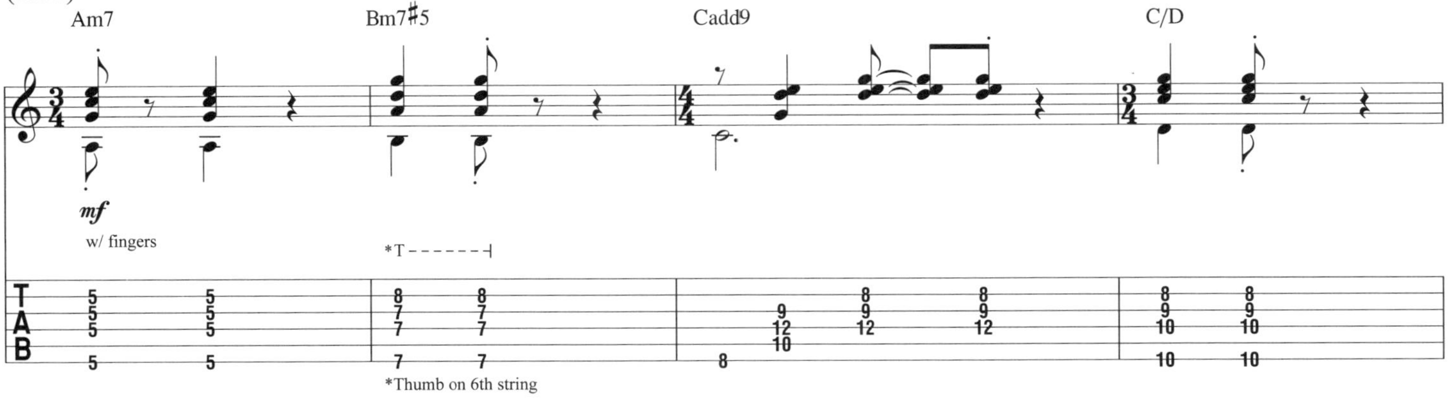

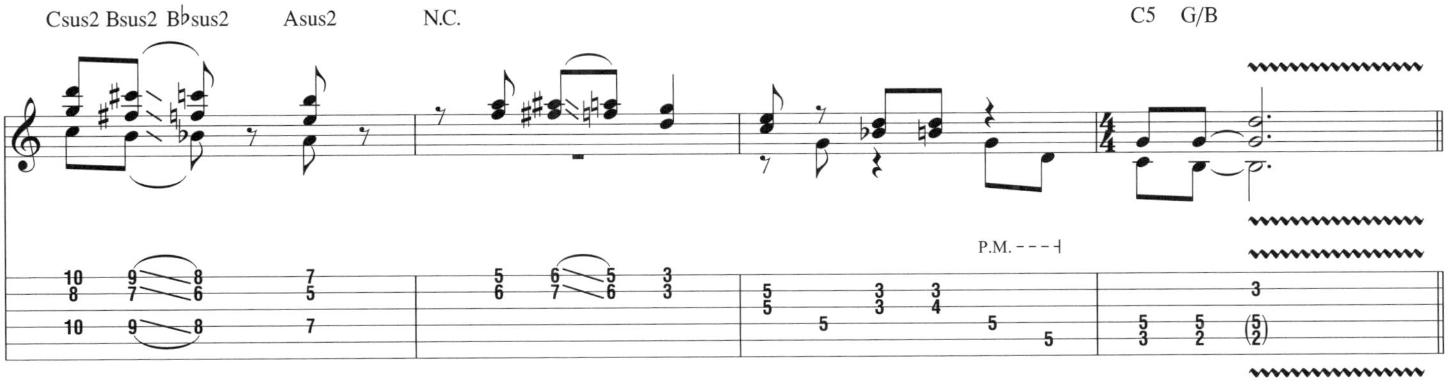

Example 18: Articulated style

(0:36)

Example 19: Fingerstyle lead
(1:01)

*Hypothetical fret location, played directly above single-coil neck pickup.

Example 20: Chords and single notes

(1:29)

Example 21: Country-style mock chicken pickin'
(2:07)

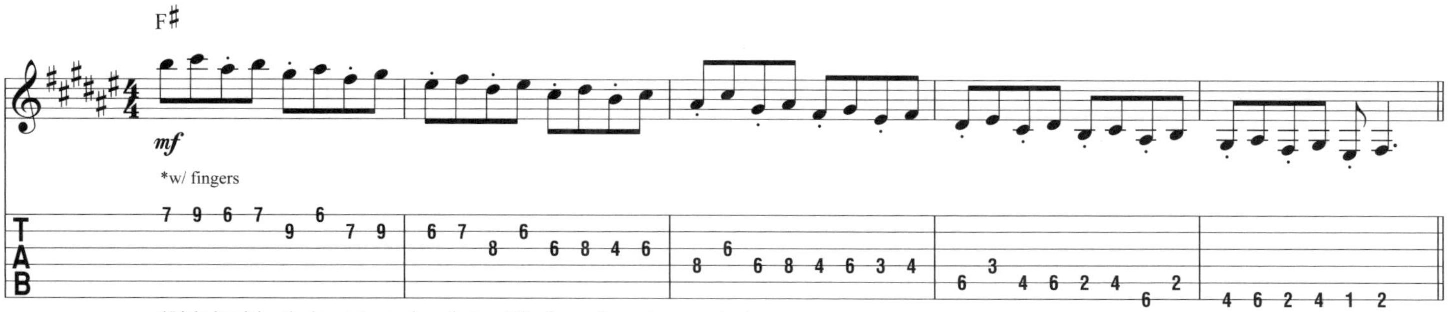

*Right-hand thumb plays notes on down-beat, middle-finger plays notes on up-beat.

Example 22: Wes Montgomery thumb octaves
(2:59)

Example 23: Wes Montgomery style
(3:20)

Example 24: Hibrid picking with bounce technique
(4:17)

Example 25 (Fig. 8 on video)
(4:41)

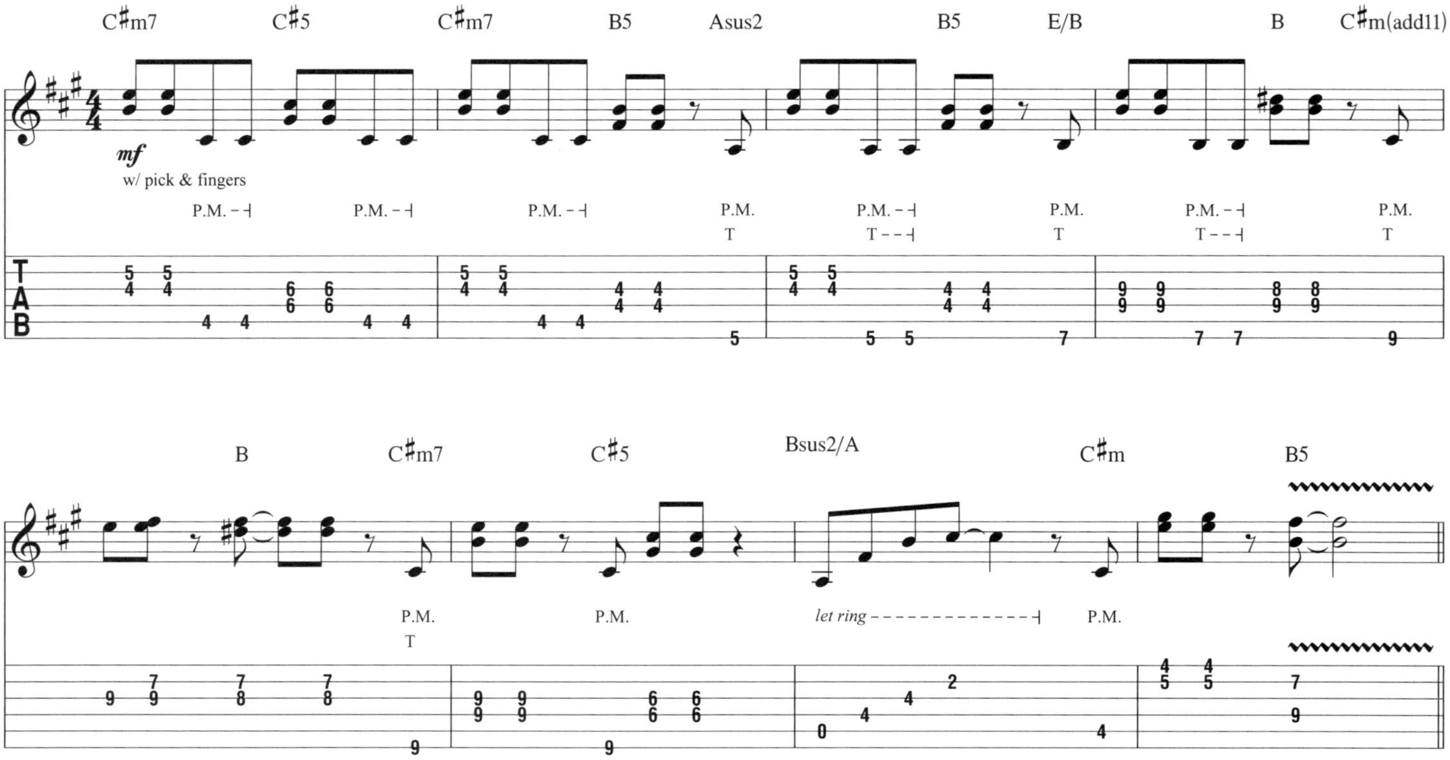

Example 26: Hibrid picking in lead style
(4:59)

Example 27: Fingerstyle with hidden pick
(5:26)

Chapter 3: Left-Hand Fingering

Example 28: Fretting two notes with one finger
(2:37)

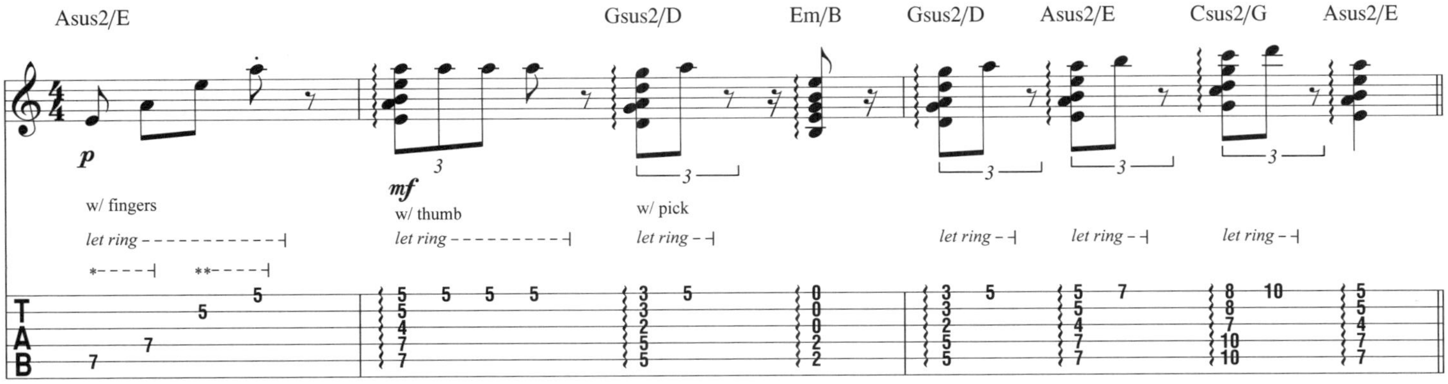

*Left-hand ring finger frets between 4th & 5th strings.
**Left-hand middle finger frets between 1st & 2nd strings.

Example 29: Fretting bottom two strings with thumb
(2:56)

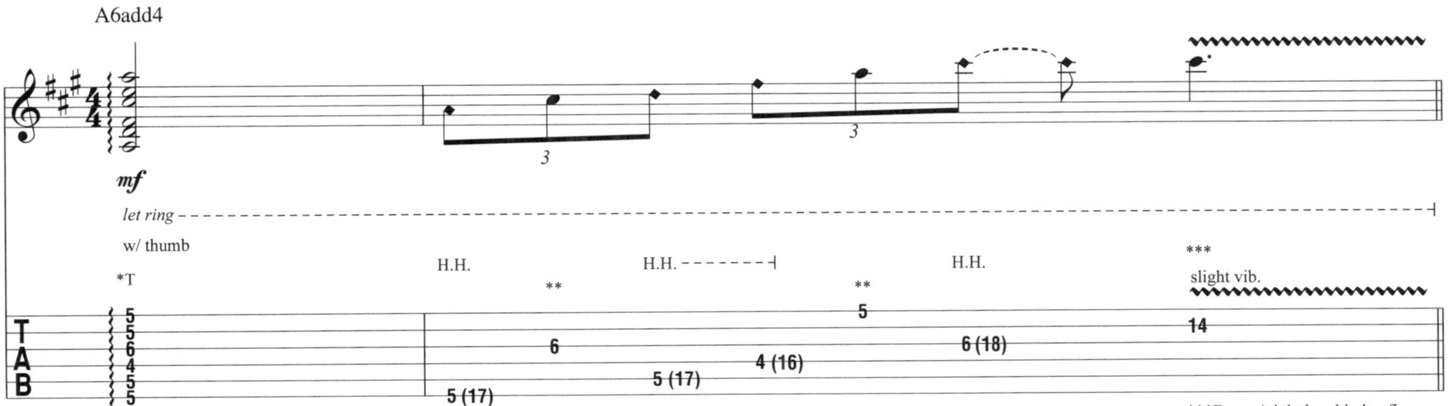

*Thumb barres 6th and 5th strings.
**Note sounded w/ right hand pinky finger.
***Fret w/ right hand index finger.

Example 30 (Fig. 9 on video): "Soulful Terrain" chord example
(3:08)

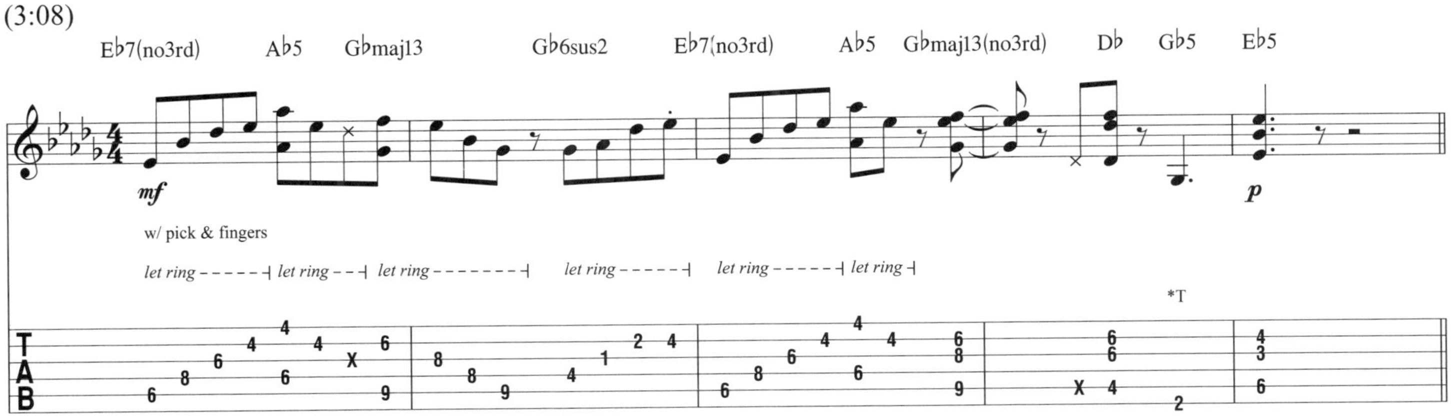

*T = Thumb on 6th string

Example 31 (Fig. 10 on video): Big-stretch chords
(3:54)

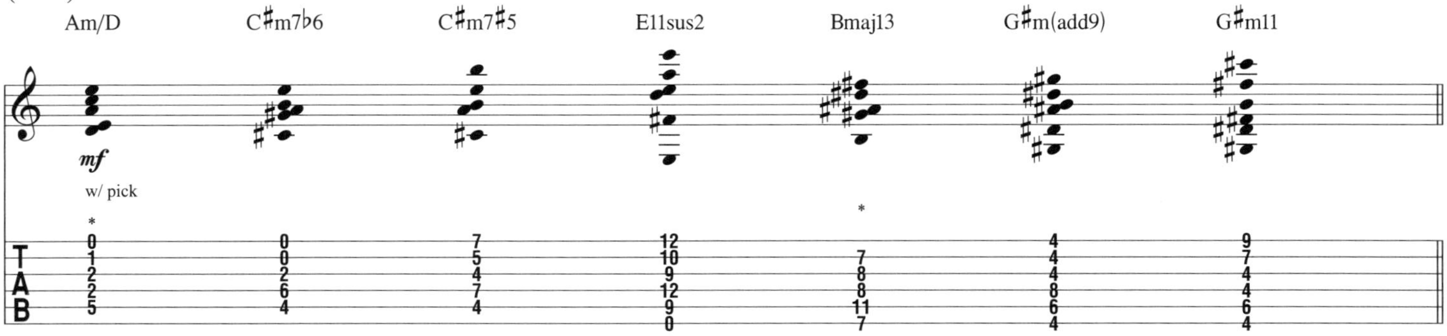

*Middle finger frets between 3rd and 4th strings.

Example 32: Thumb behind the neck to facilitate fast lead passages
(4:48)

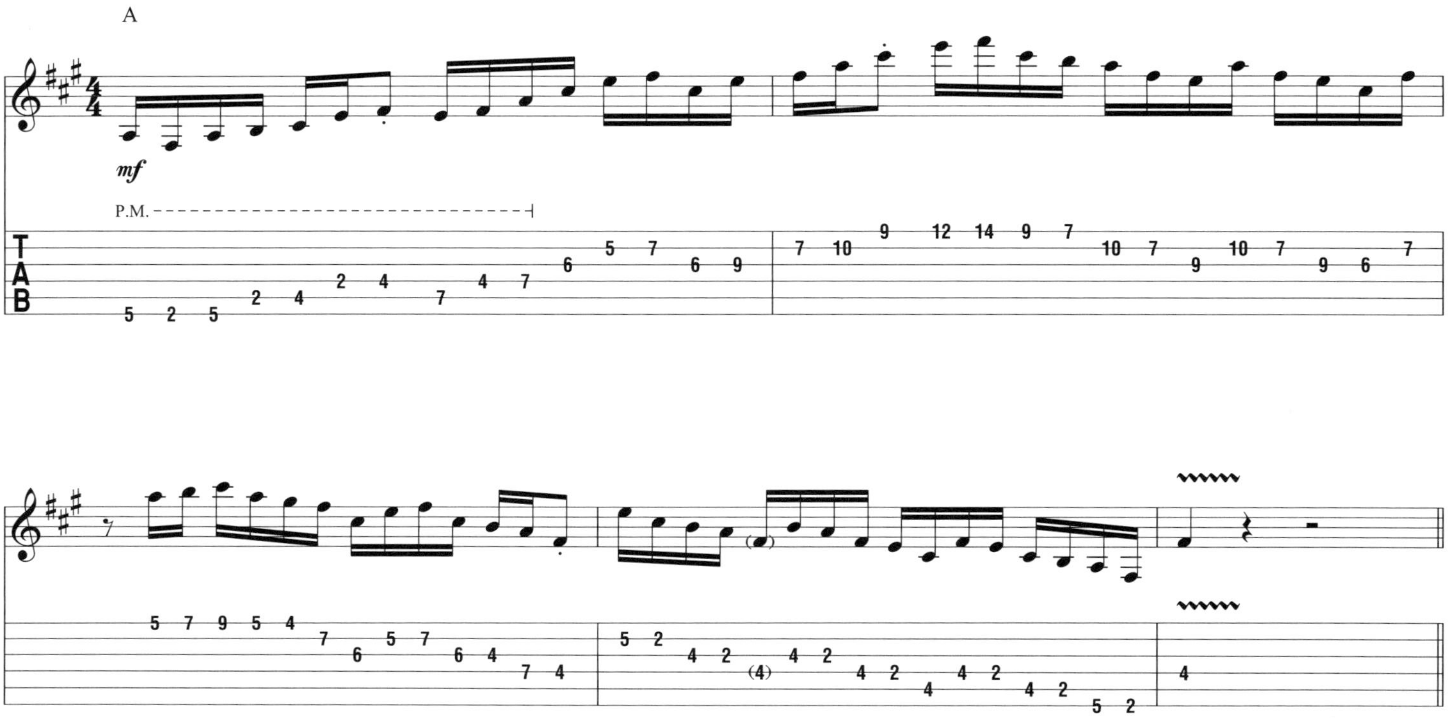

Example 33
(4:57)

Example 34 (Fig. 11 on video): Jimi Hendrix style
(6:55)

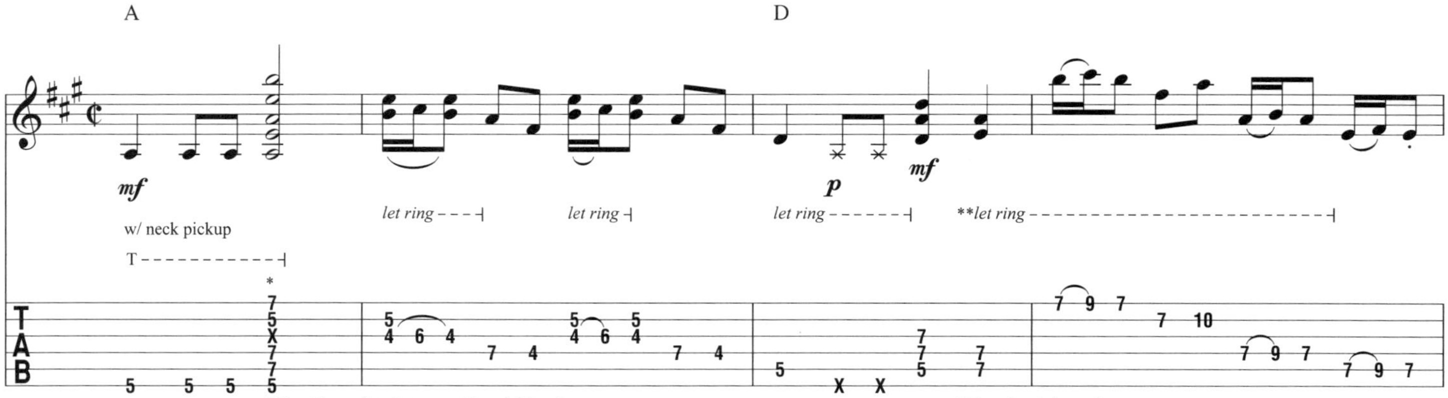

*Ring finger frets between 4th and 5th strings.

**Let chord ring only.

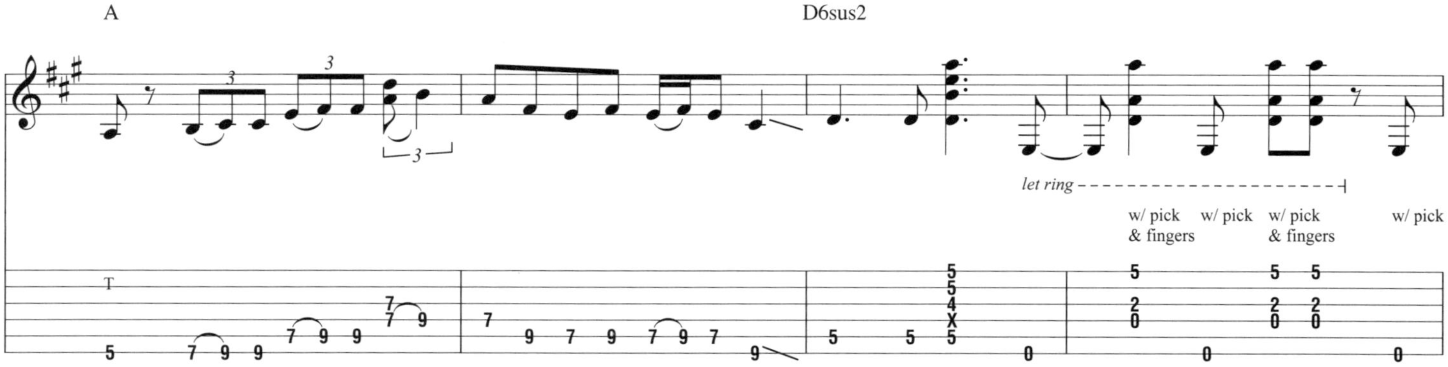

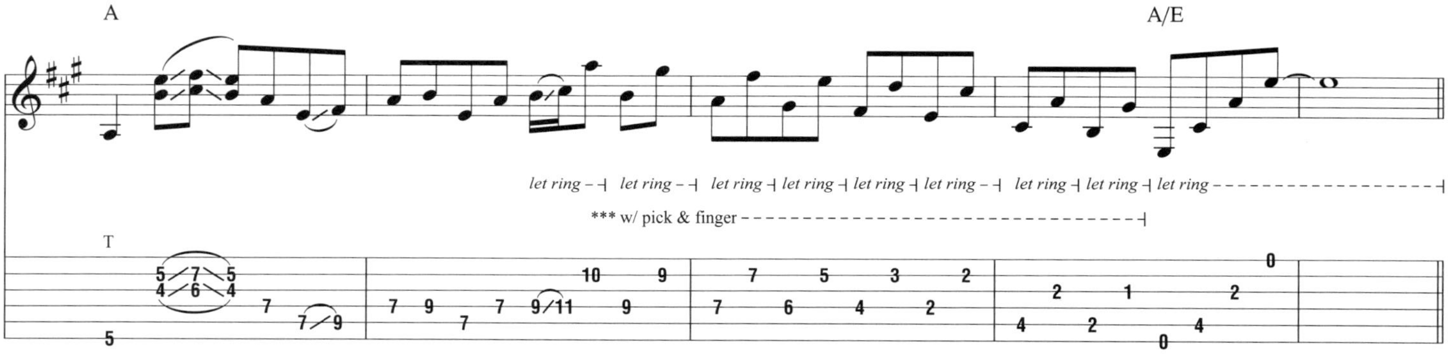

***Pick plays notes on 4th & 5th strings, middle fingers plays notes on 2nd and 3rd strings.

Chapter 4: Left-Hand Muting

Example 35: Left-hand muting
(1:52)

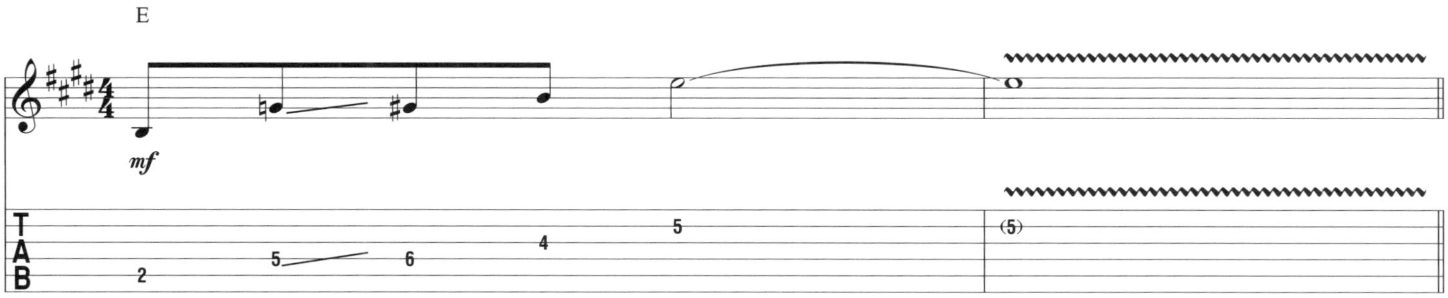

Example 36: Two-hand muting
(2:39)

Example 37: Muting while using legato technique
(3:22)

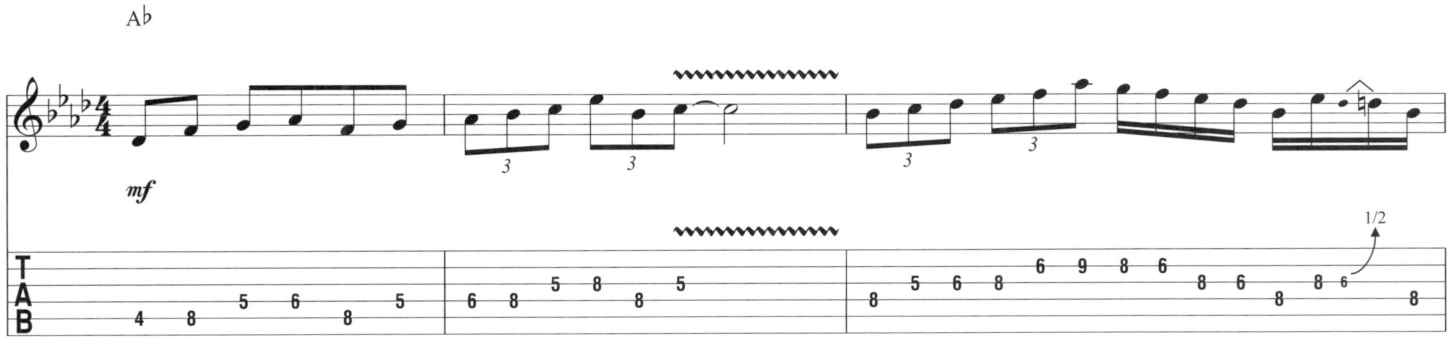

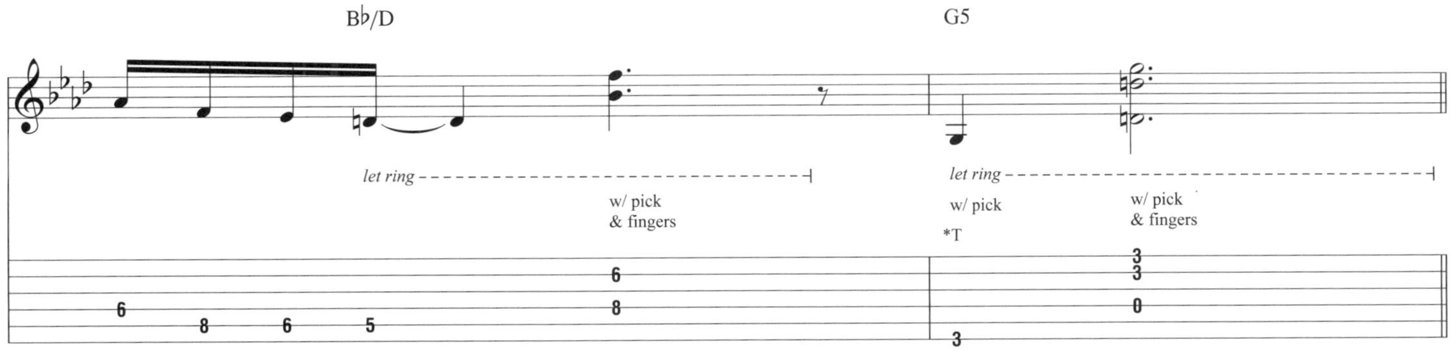

*T = Thumb on 6th string

Example 38: Muting for fast runs
(3:40)

Example 39A
(5:28)

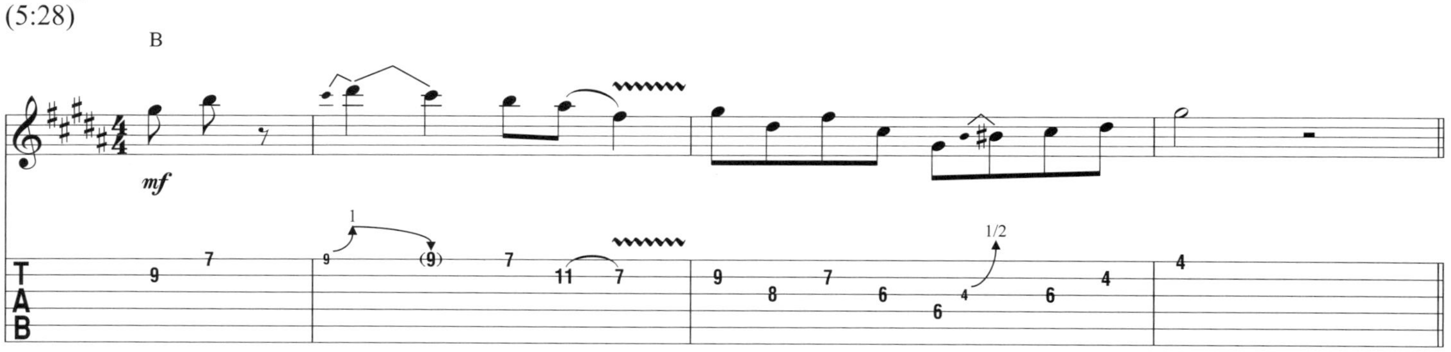

Example 39B
(5:33)

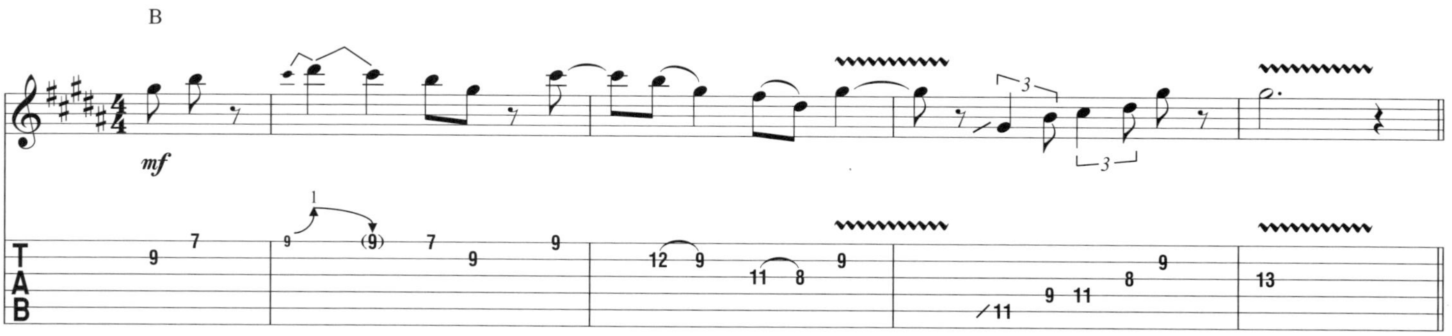

Example 39C
(5:40)

Chapter 5: Chords

Example 40 (Fig. 12 on video): Basic chord progression
(2:38)

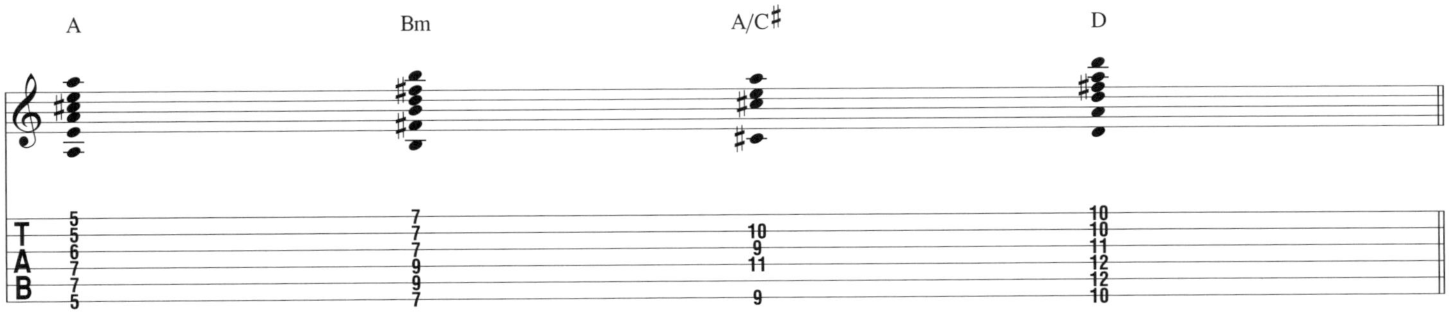

Example 41 (Fig. 13 on video): Basic chord progression variation 1
(3:01)

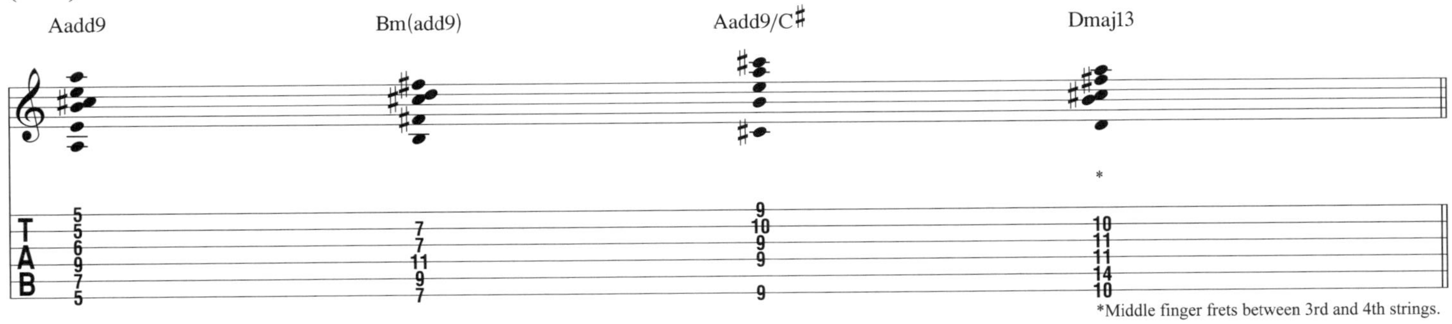

*Middle finger frets between 3rd and 4th strings.

Example 42 (Fig. 14 on video): Basic chord progression variation 2
(3:20)

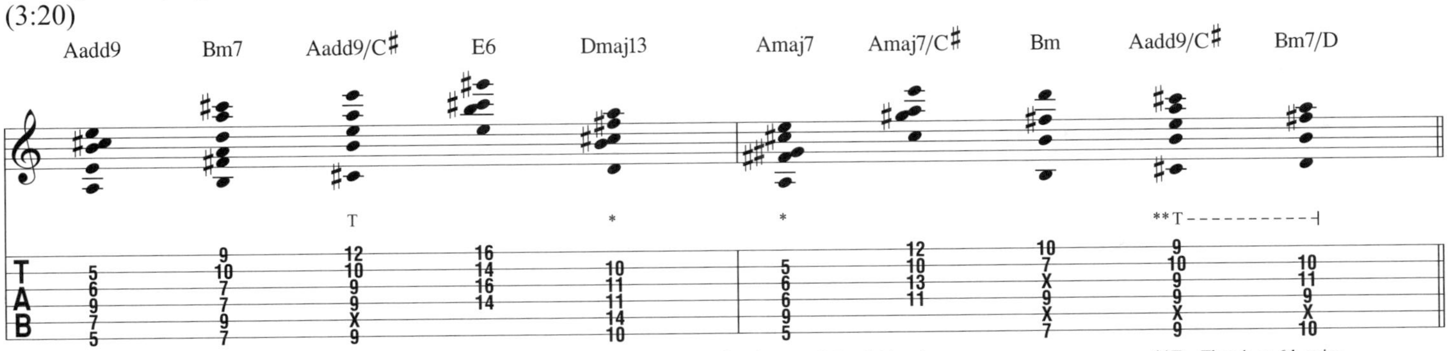

*Middle finger frets between 3rd and 4th strings.

**T = Thumb on 6th string

Example 43: Chord melody
(3:41)

Example 44 (Fig. 15 on video): D chord variations
(4:22)

Example 45 (Fig. 16 on video): More D chord variations
(4:54)

Example 46 (Fig. 16A on video): More D chord variations
(5:16)

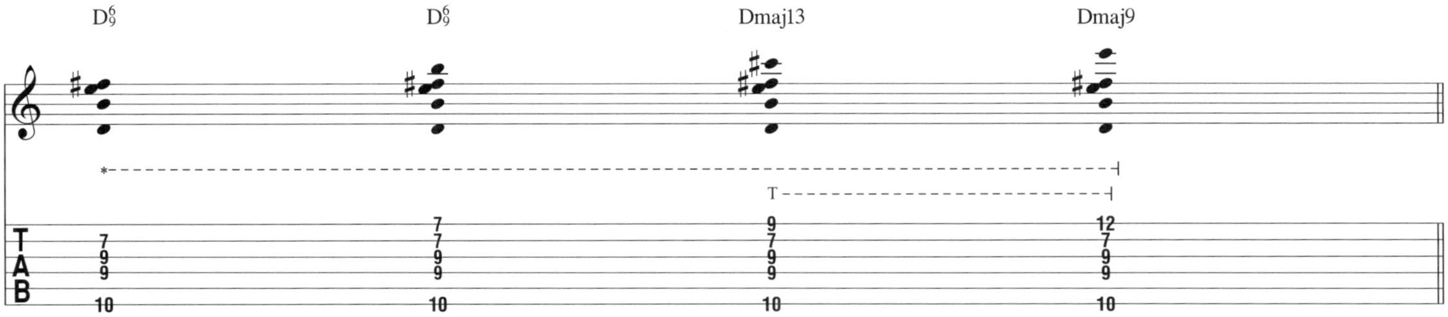

*Middle finger frets 3rd and 4th strings.

Example 47: Power chord sounds
(5:47)

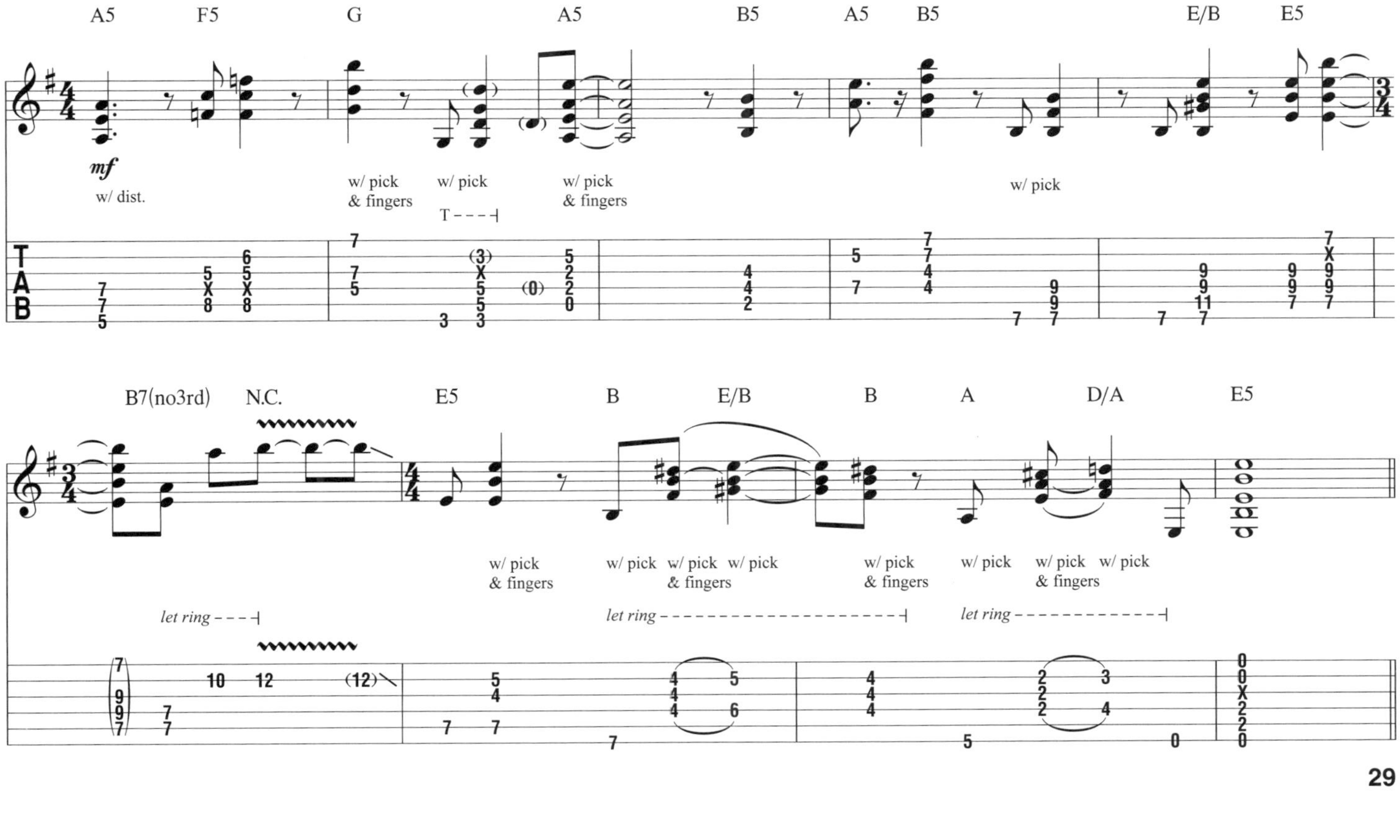

Chapter 6: Chord Techniques of EJ's Influences

Example 48: Jimi Hendrix chord style

(0:38)

Example 49 (Fig. 17 on video): Jimi Hendrix chord style
(1:18)

Example 50: Jimi Hendrix “Axis” style
(2:10)

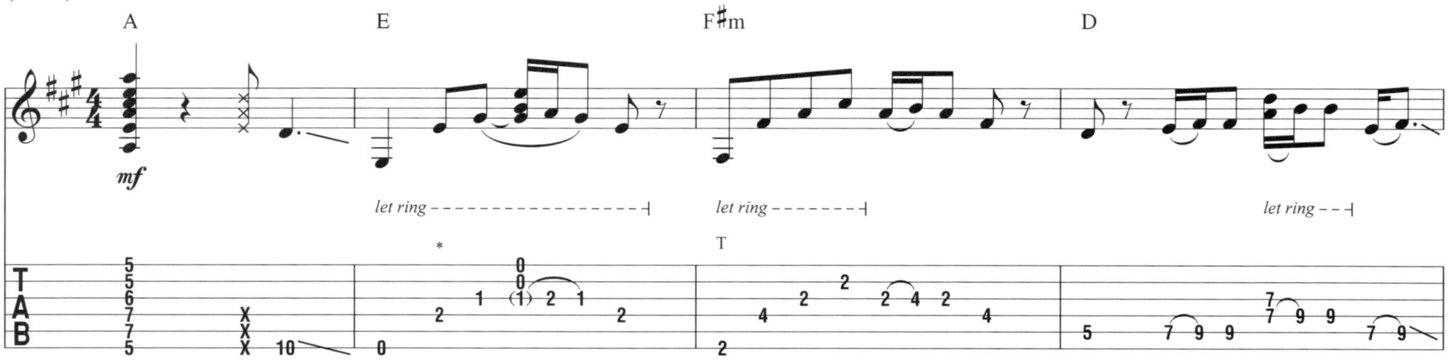

*Note does not ring.

Example 51: Jimi Hendrix “Ladyland” style
(2:28)

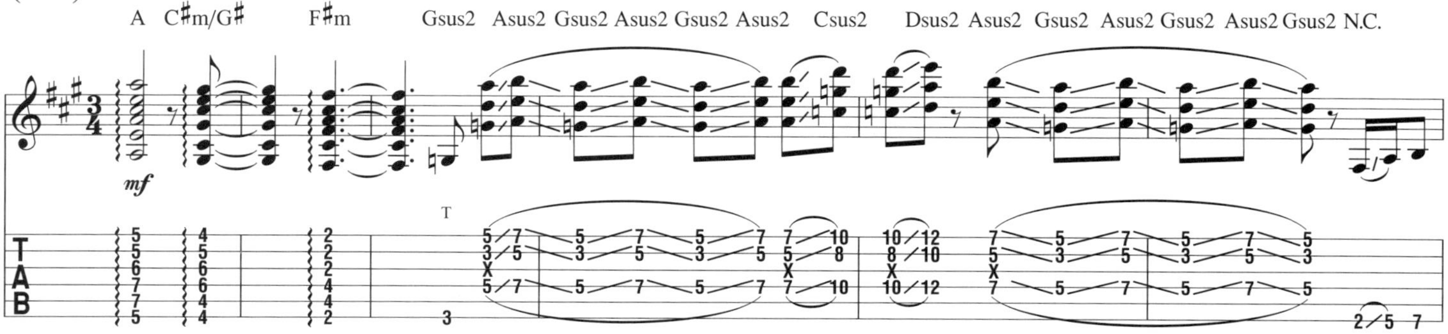

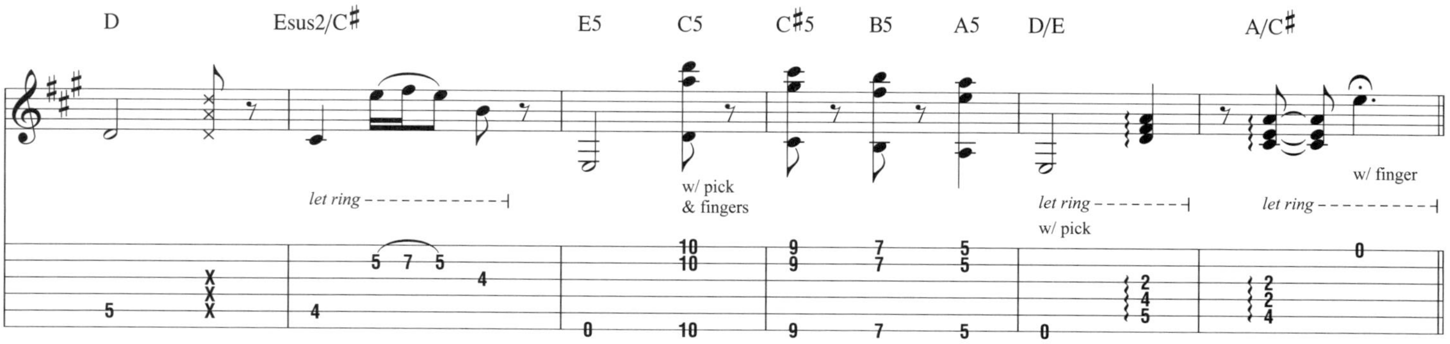

Example 52 (Fig. 18 on video): Wes Montgomery thumb strumming chords
(3:04)

Example 53 (Fig. 19 on video): Chet Atkins style
(4:43)

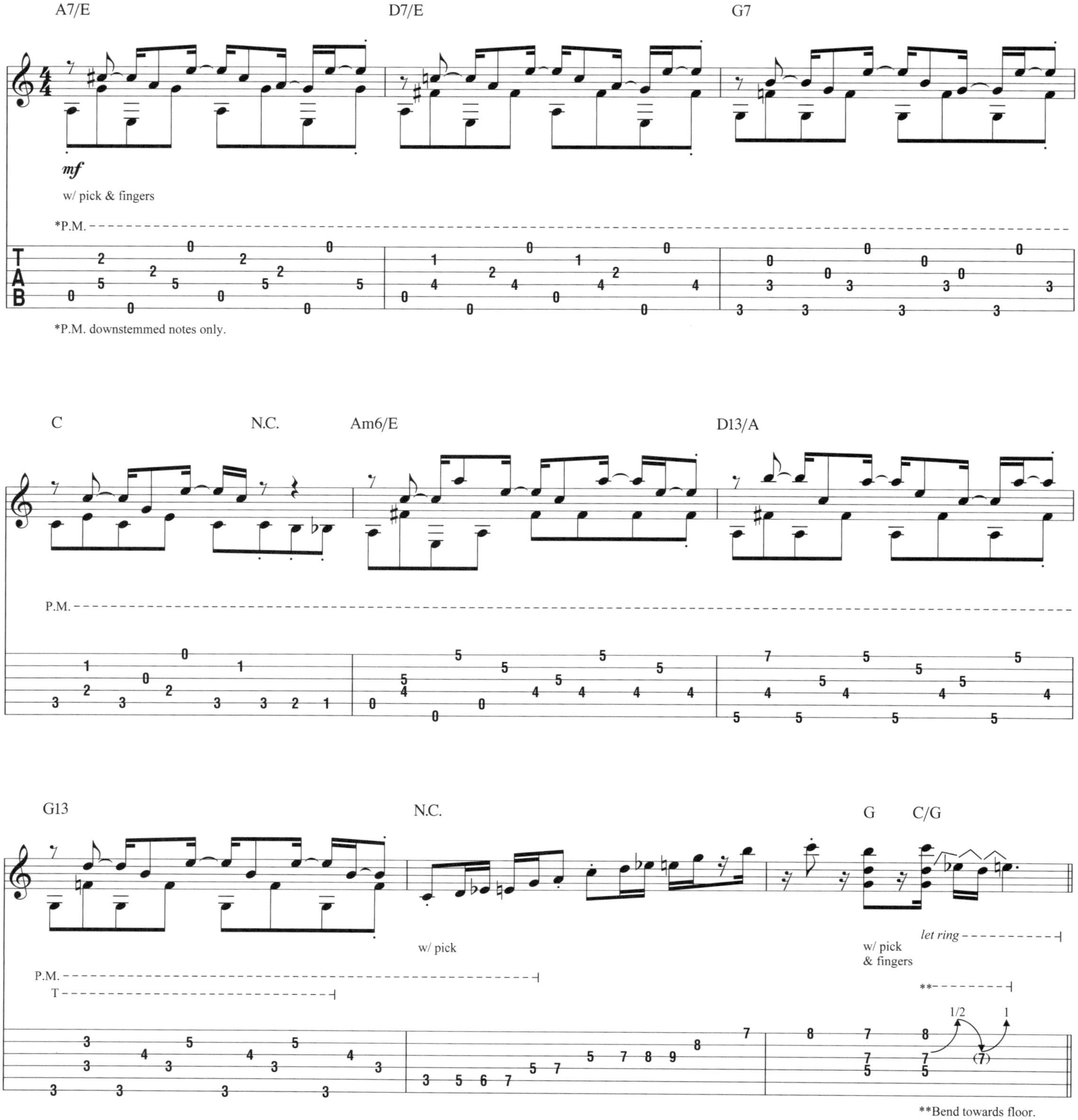

Example 54: Chet Atkins style with melody
(5:05)

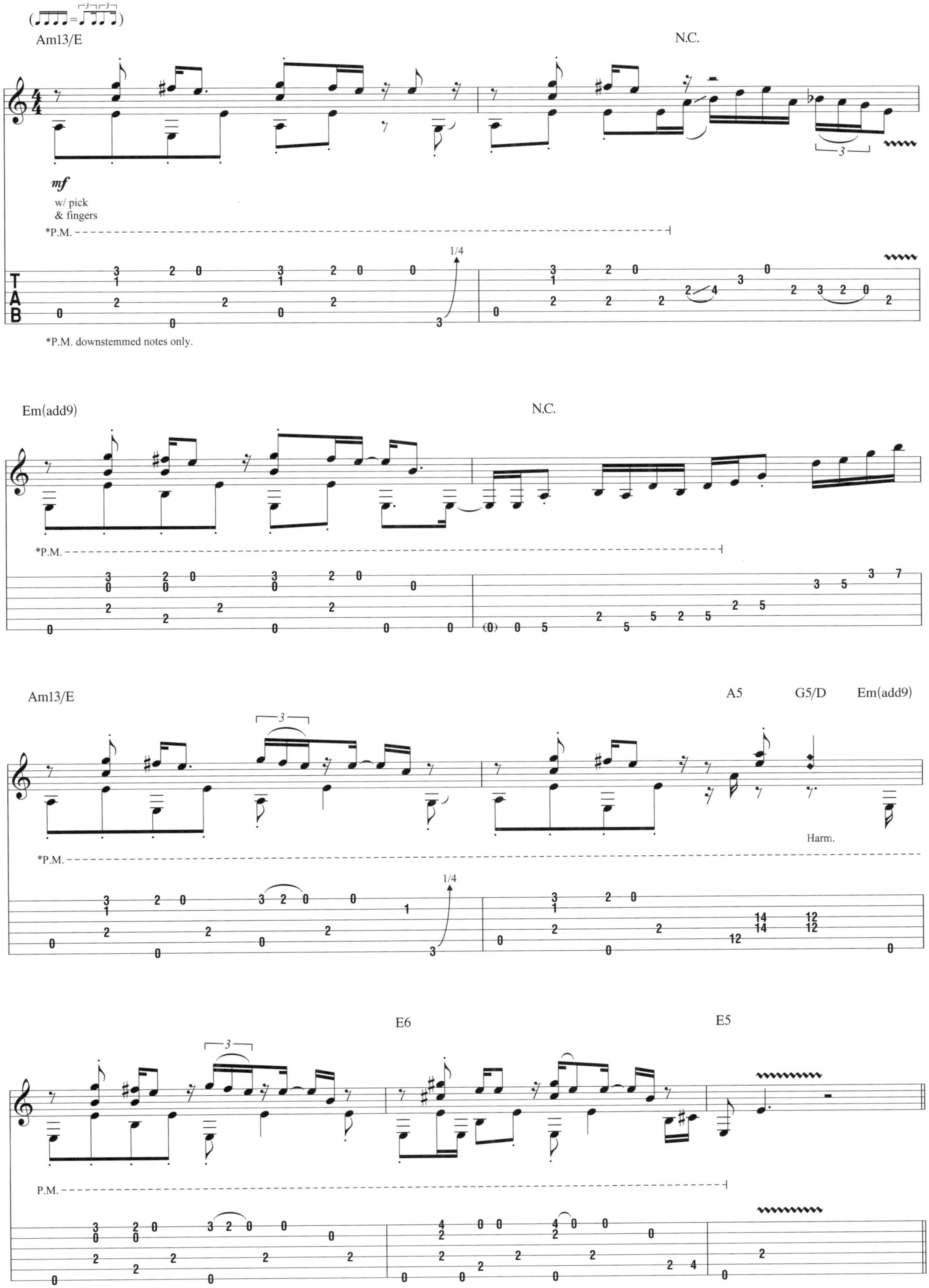

Example 55 (Fig. 2 on video): Jerry Reed style

(6:29)

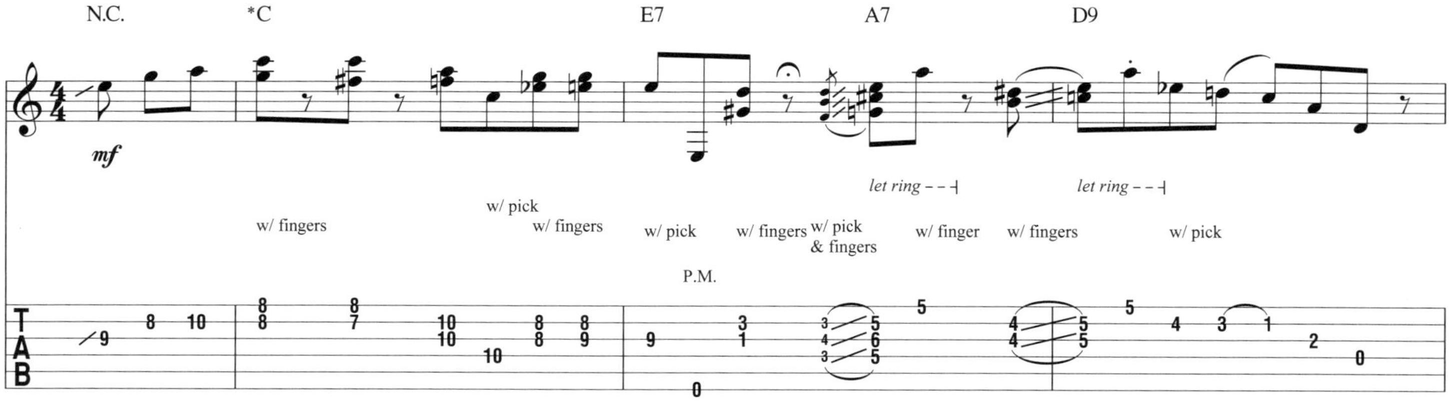

*Chord symbols reflect implied harmony.

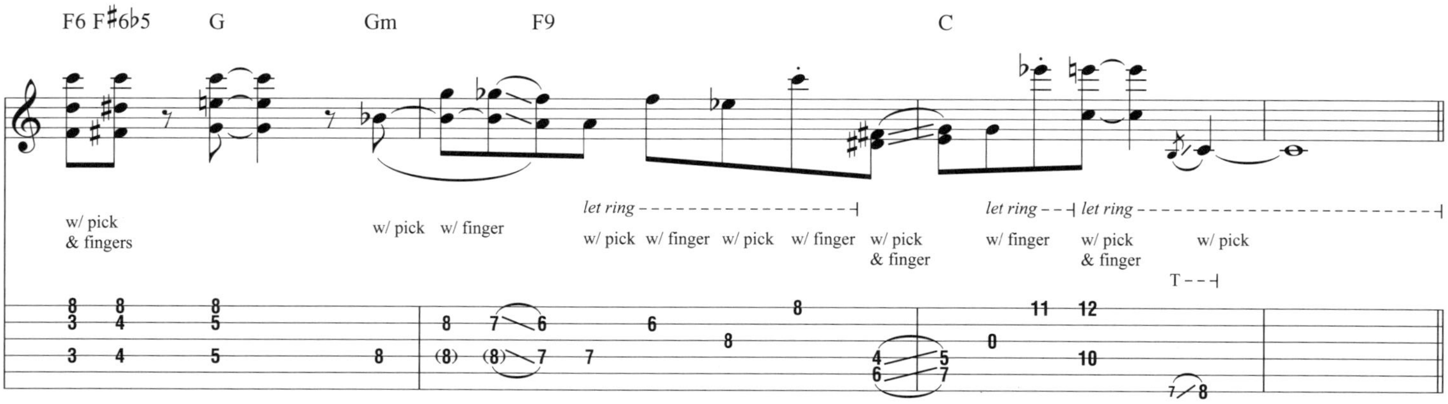

Example 56 (Fig. 21 on video): Jerry Reed style variation
(7:01)

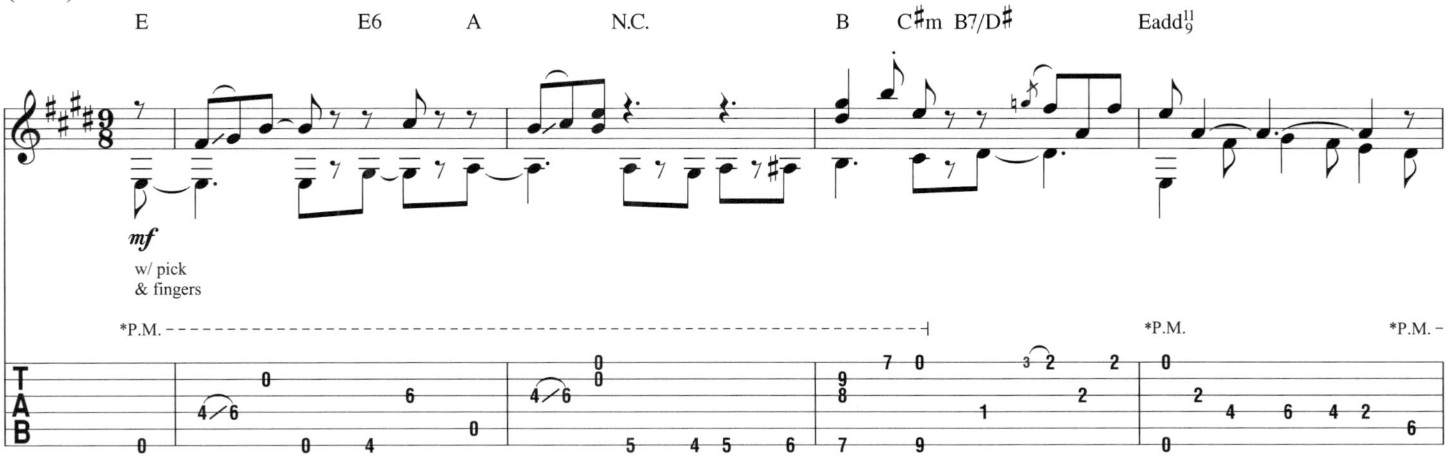

*P.M. downstemmed notes only.

Example 57 (Fig. 22 on video): Keith Richards style
(8:39)

Chapter 7: Lead Guitar

Example 58 (Fig. 23 on video): Pentatonic-based line
(0:23)

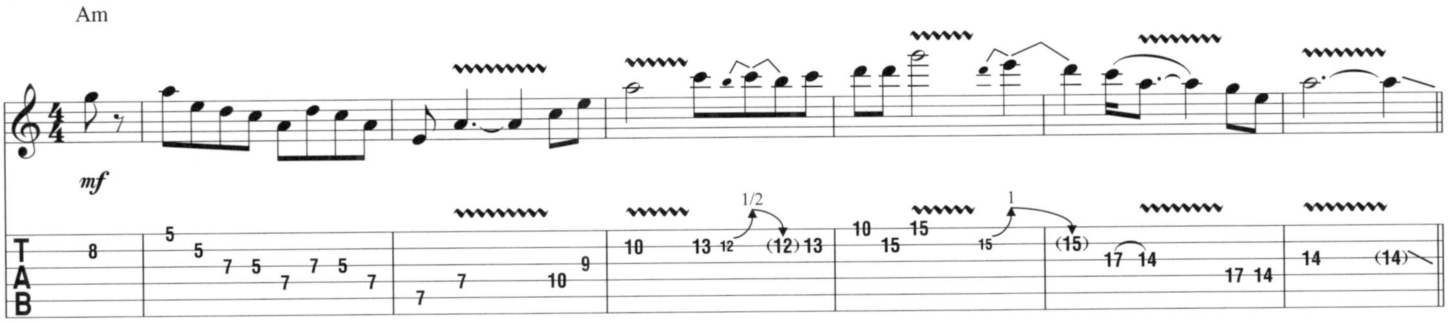

Example 59: Pentatonic with added 2nd
(0:37)

Example 60: Pentatonic with added 6th
(0:48)

Example 61 (Fig. 24 on video): Pentatonic with added 2nd and 6th
(1:02)

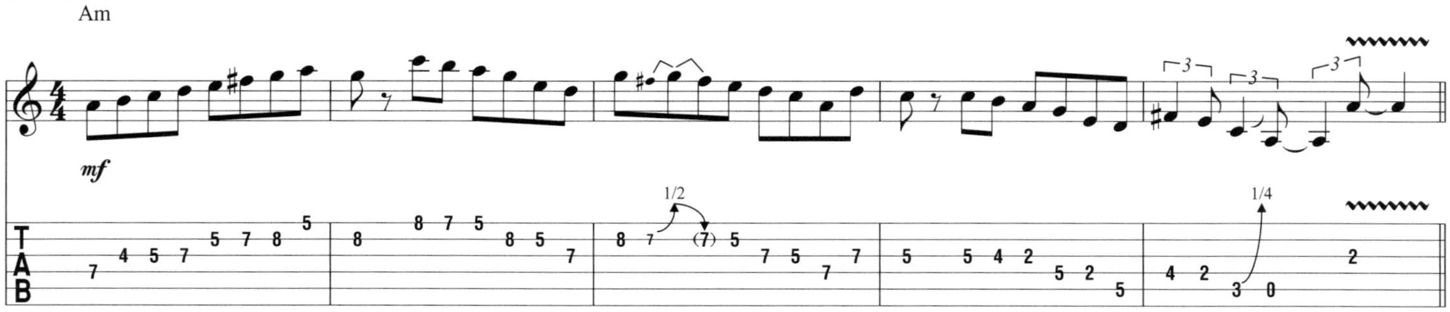

Example 62 (Fig. 25 on video): Mixing pentatonic scales
(1:54)

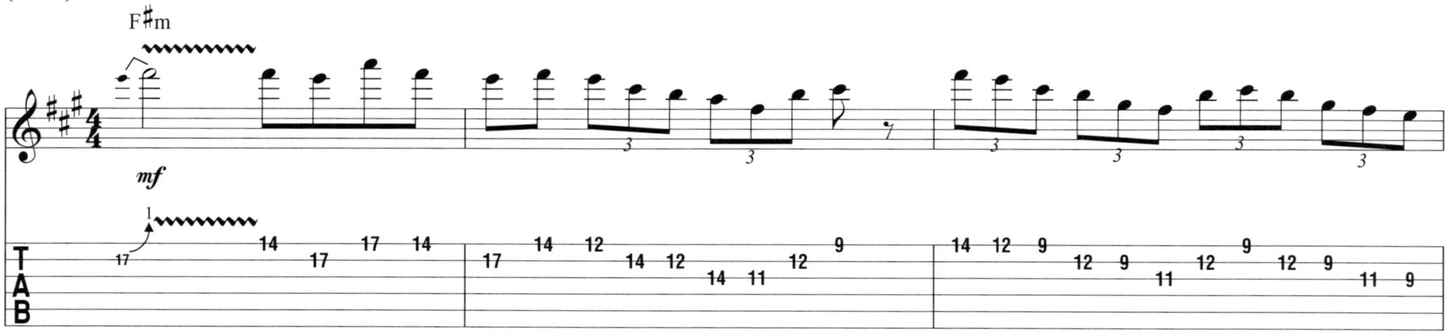

Example 63: Mixing more pentatonic scales
(2:09)

Example 64: More mixing scales
(2:27)

Example 65 (Fig. 26 on video): Combining B minor pentatonic and A minor scales
(2:47)

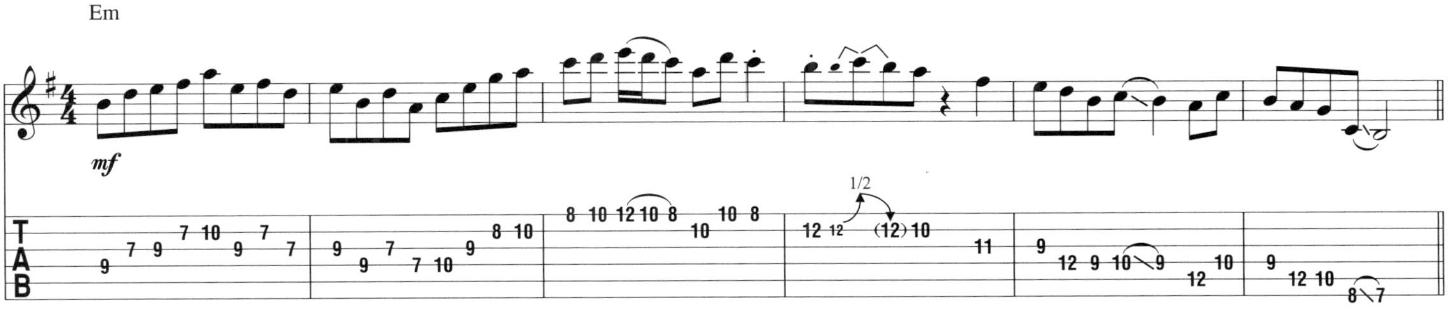

Example 66: Using dyads to create lead lines
(3:11)

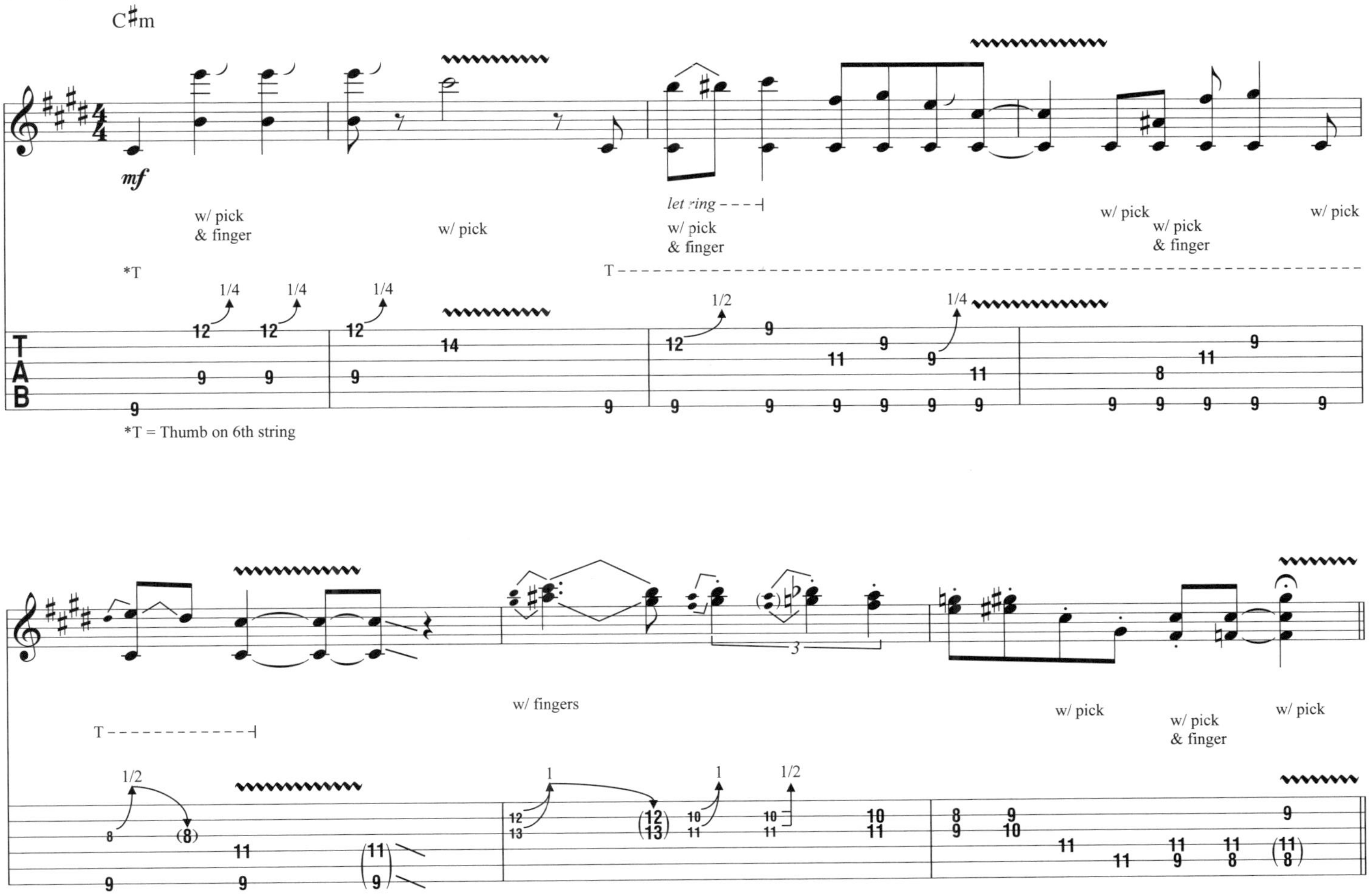

Example 67 (Fig. 27 on video): Using 3rds and 4ths dyads in lead lines
(3:29)

Example 68: Using accents

(4:27)

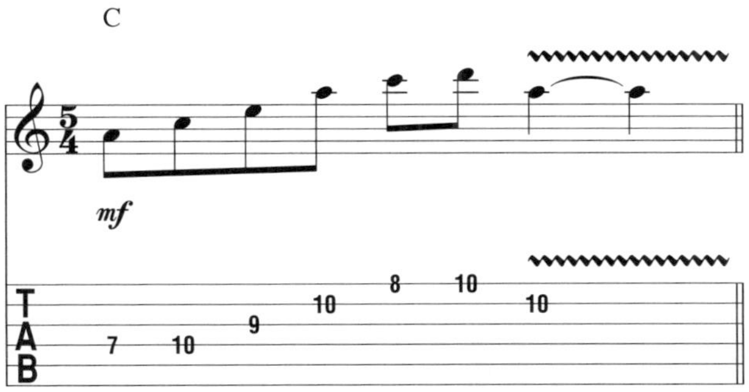

(4:33)

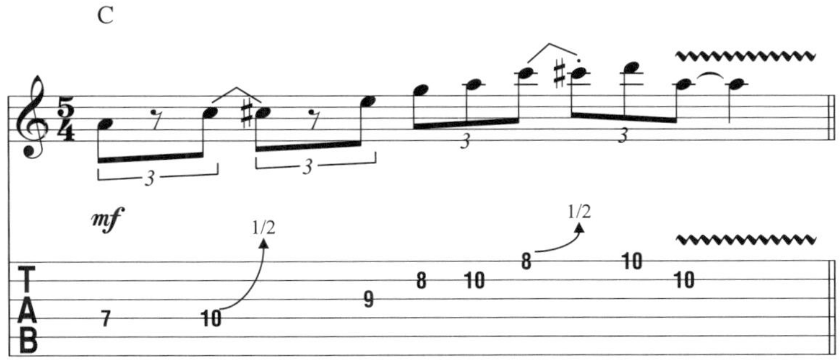

Example 69: Adding nuance

(4:40)

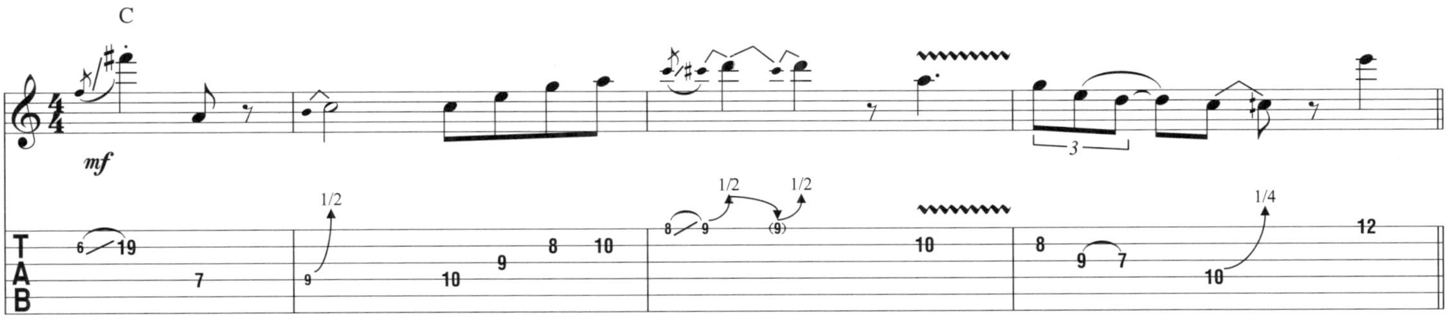

Example 70: Adding color and sass

(4:53)

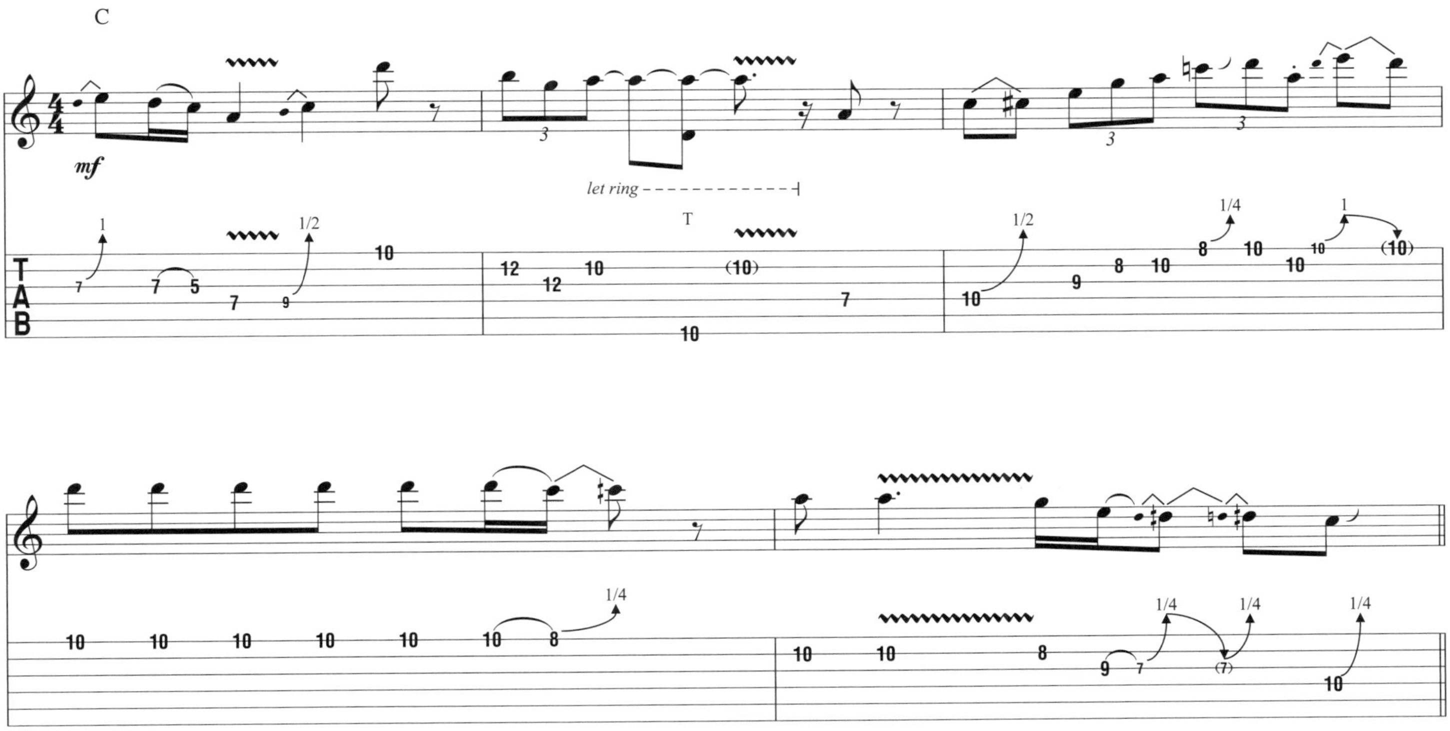

Chapter 8: Lead Guitar Influences

Example 71: Clapton-style line

(0:30)

Example 72 (Fig. 28 on video): The Clapton influence
(1:07)

Example 73: Clapton's subtle vibrato

(2:15)

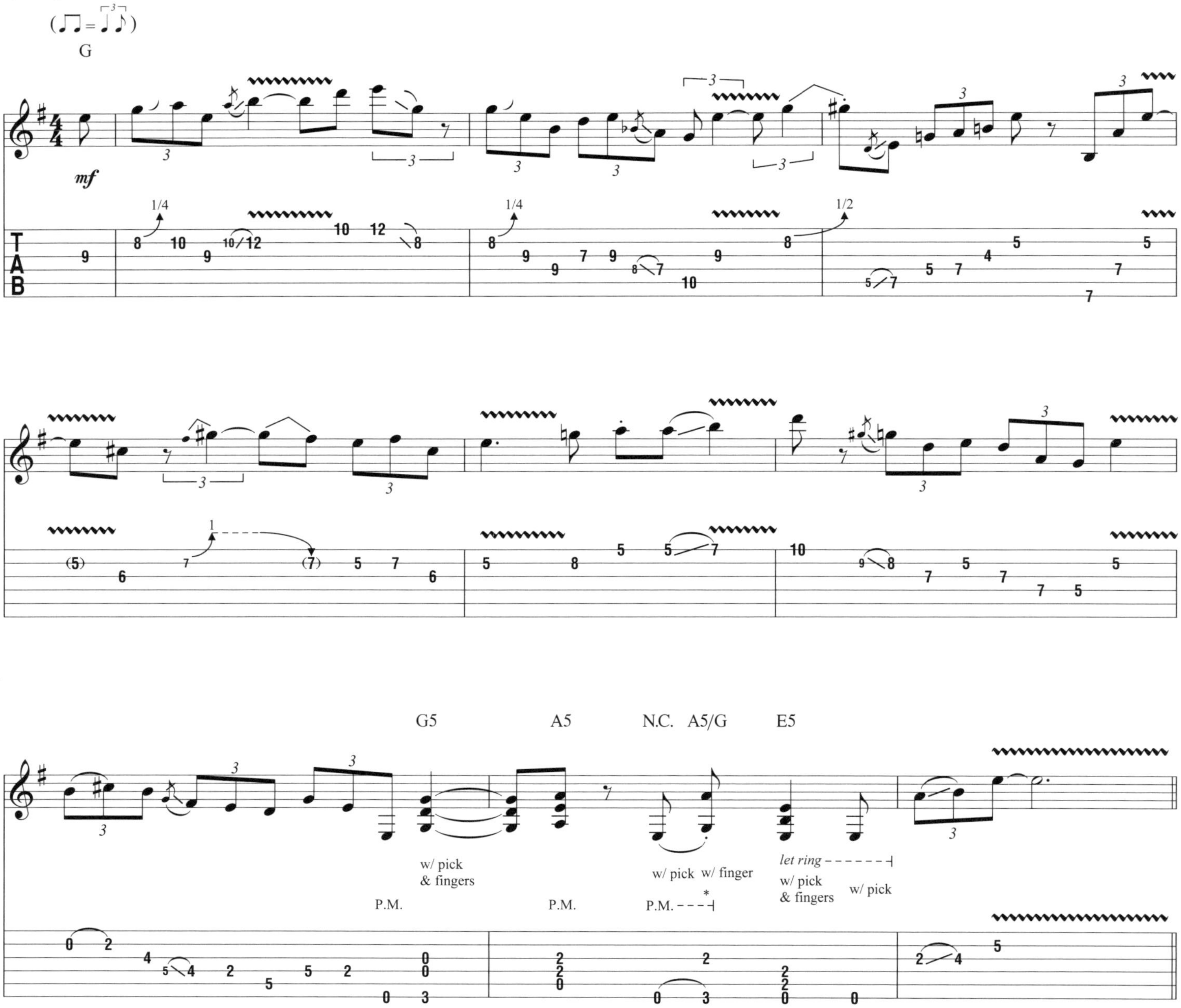

*P.M. applies to 6th string only.

Example 74 (Fig. 29 on video): Clapton's bigger vibrato
(2:45)

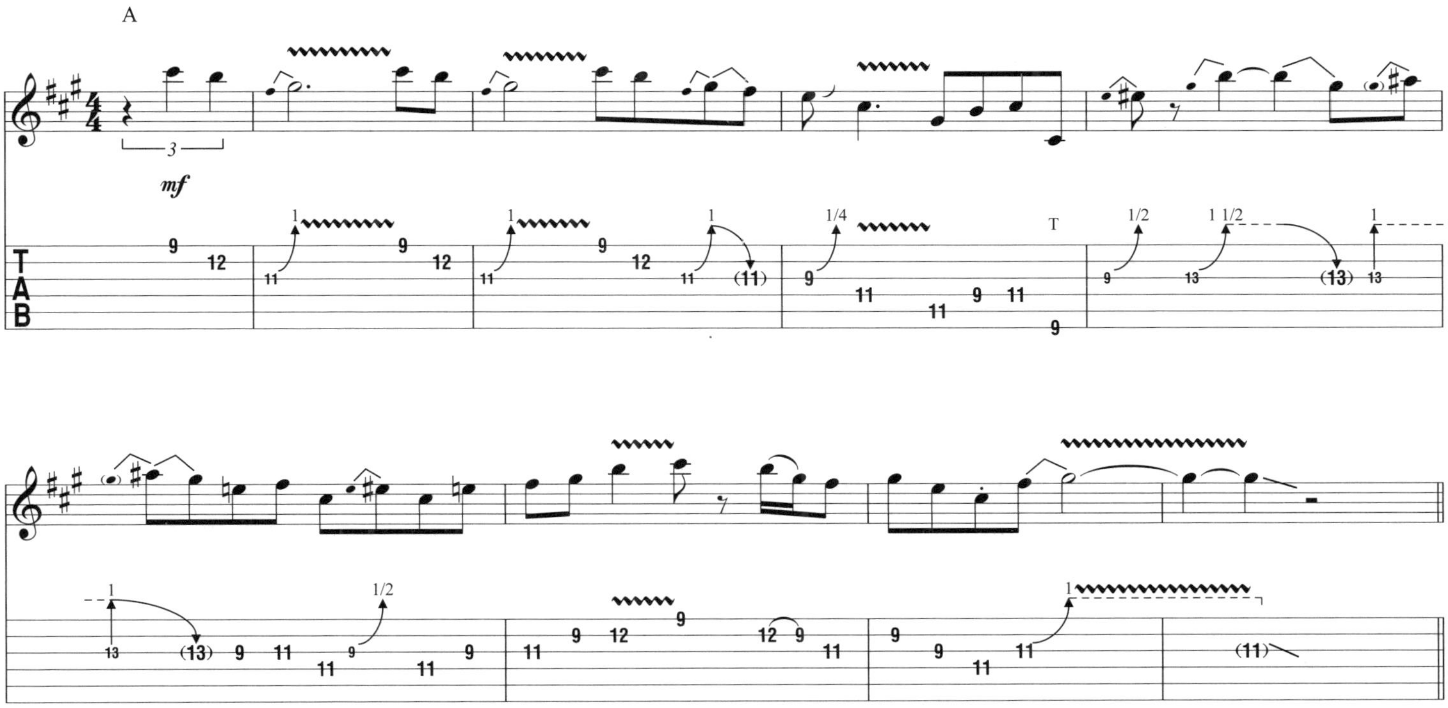

Example 75: Jeff Beck's use of semitones
(4:07)

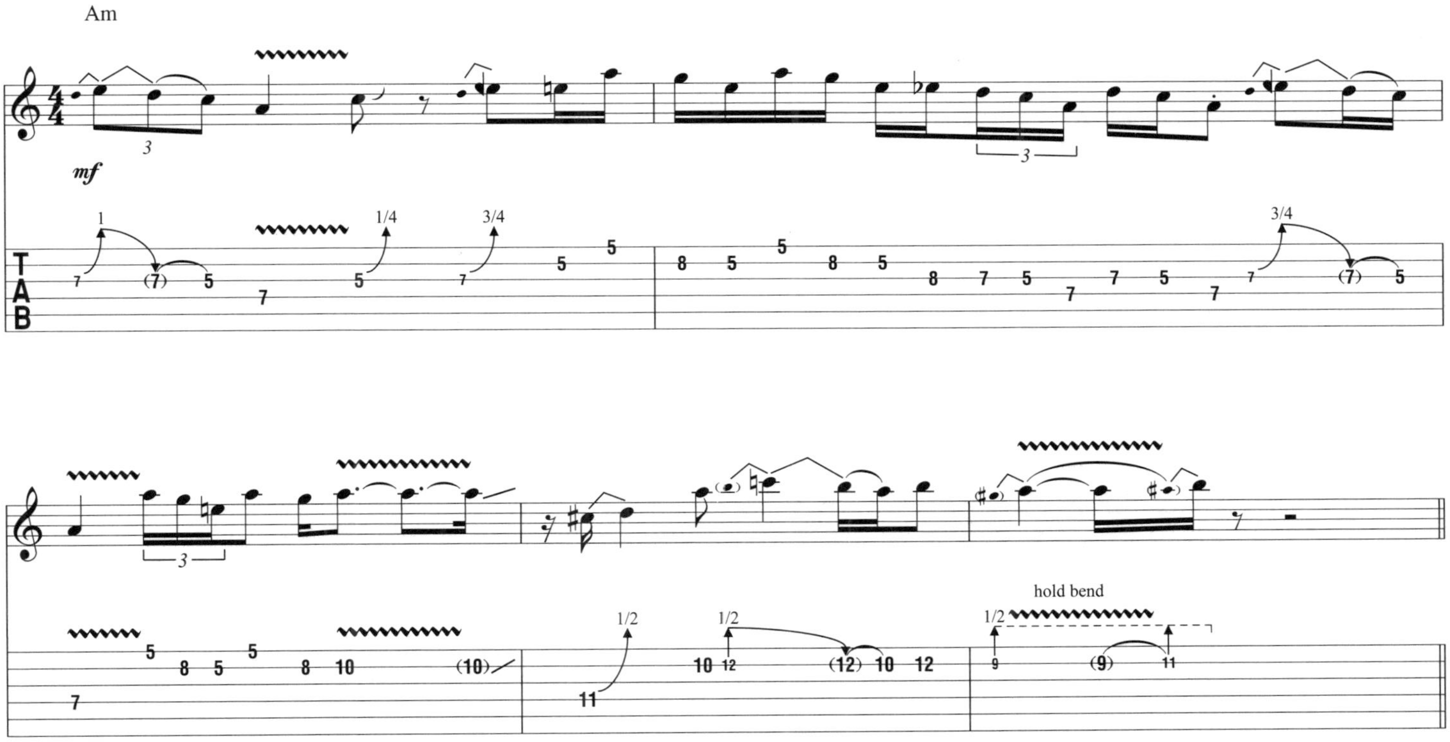

Example 76: Jeff Beck style of ending a line with tension
(5:02)

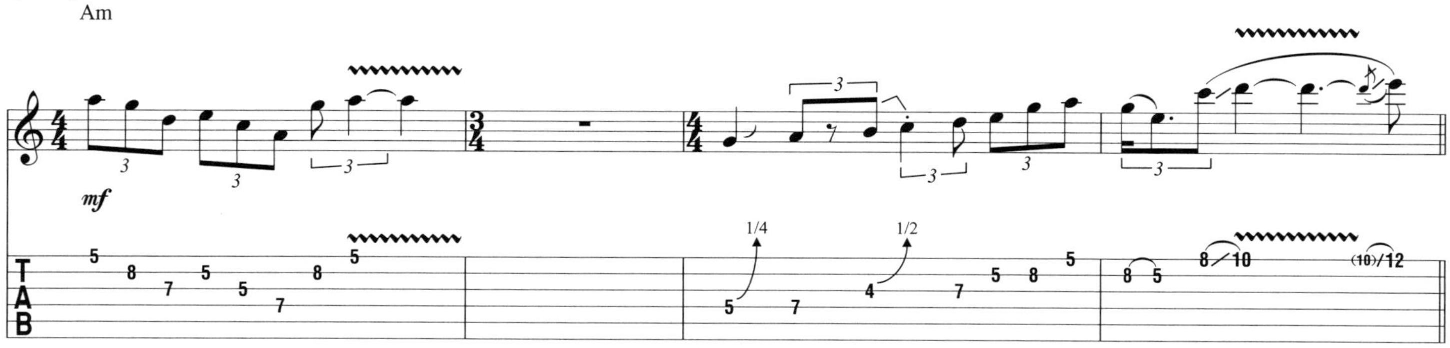

Example 77: Jeff Beck style line emulating a pitch wheel
(5:24)

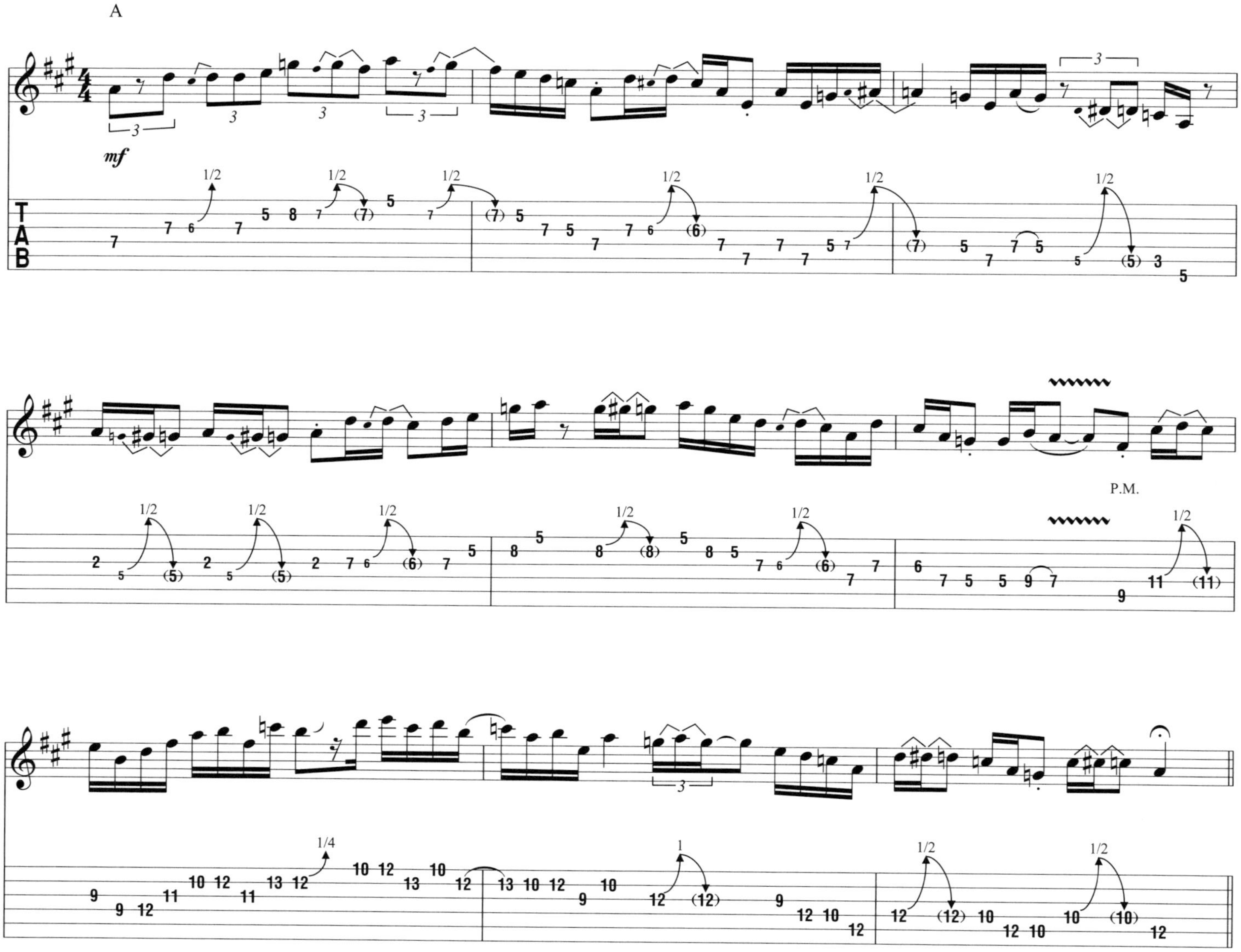

Example 78 (Fig. 30 on video): Jeff Beck microbends to emulate a pitch wheel
(5:48)

Example 79: Jimi Hendrix blues-based lead style
(6:34)

Example 80: Jimi Hendrix "Red House" style
(7:06)

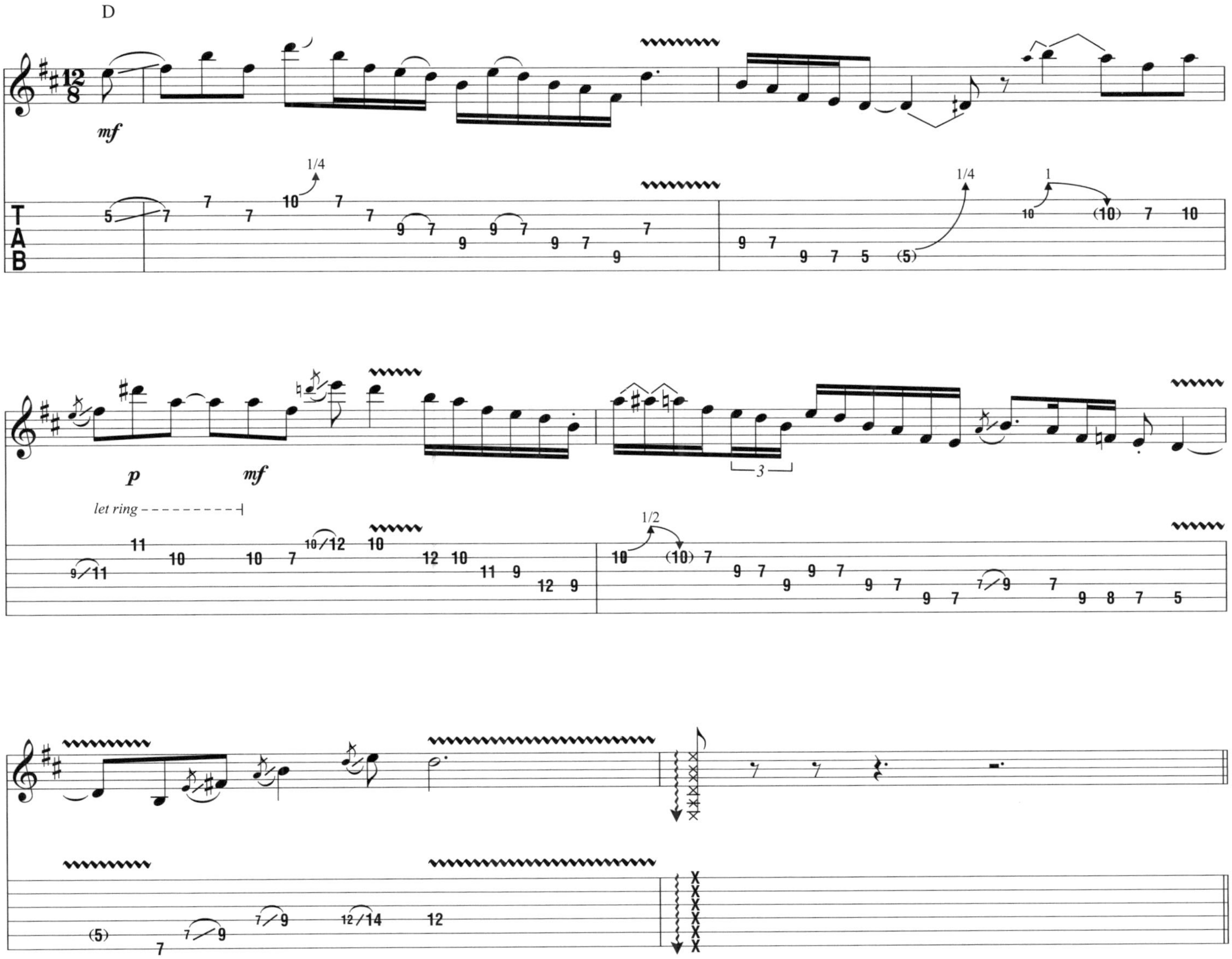

Example 81 (Fig. 31 on video): Jimi Hendrix bending style
(8:23)

Example 82: Chet Atkins melody within chords and bass lines
(9:20)

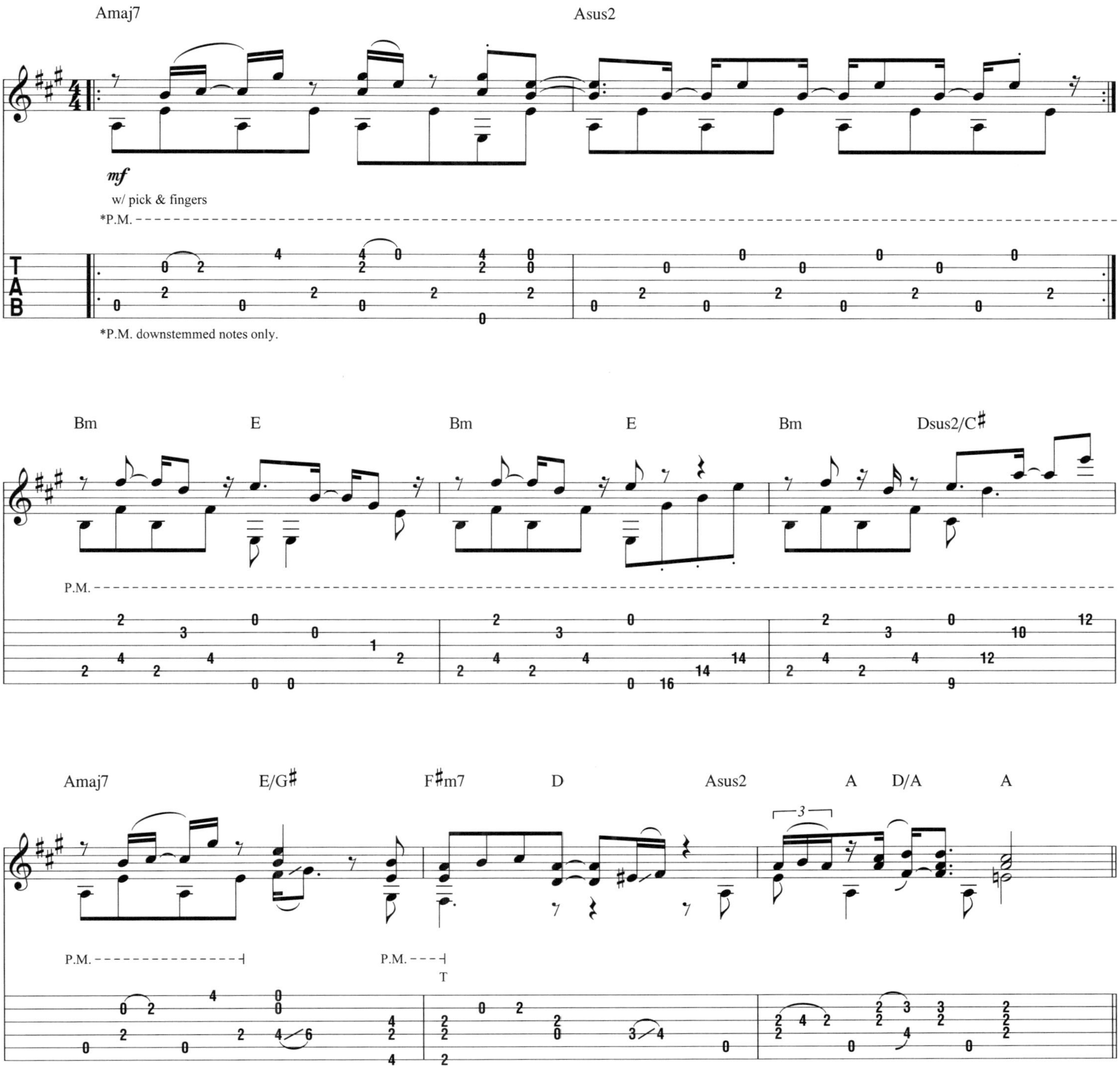

Example 83 (Fig. 32 on video): Steel guitar style string bending
(11:25)

Example 84 (Fig. 33 on video): Steel guitar style with pre-bends
(11:56)

Example 85: Country style lead using bounce and piano techniques
(12:50)

P.M.
P.M.
P.M.
let ring
1/4
slight P.M.
slight P.M.
P.M.
1/2
let ring
1
let ring
1/2
1/2
1
1/2
1

Example 86 (Fig. 34 on video): Country pedal steel guitar style
(13:32)

Example 87 (Fig. 35 on video): Wes Montgomery style lead guitar
(14:38)

Eadd9/11/G♯
F♯m6♯5
F♯m13♭5
Bm♭13
G♯m6♯5
F♯m7
B7♭9
N.C.
T
P.M.
P.M.
P.M.
*Right-hand thumb or middle-finger plays single note lines.
G♯m6♯5
F♯m7
E
N.C.
P.M.
C♯m7/G♯
F♯m7
B7sus4
B
B6
B11/A
B6
B11/A
w/ fingers
T
T
N.C.
C♯m7
A7/F♯
N.C.
F♯m
w/ thumb
w/ fingers

Example 88: Wes Montgomery style octaves
(16:35)

Chapter 9: Harmonics

Example 89: "Ping" harmonics 12 frets higher than the fretted note
(0:17)

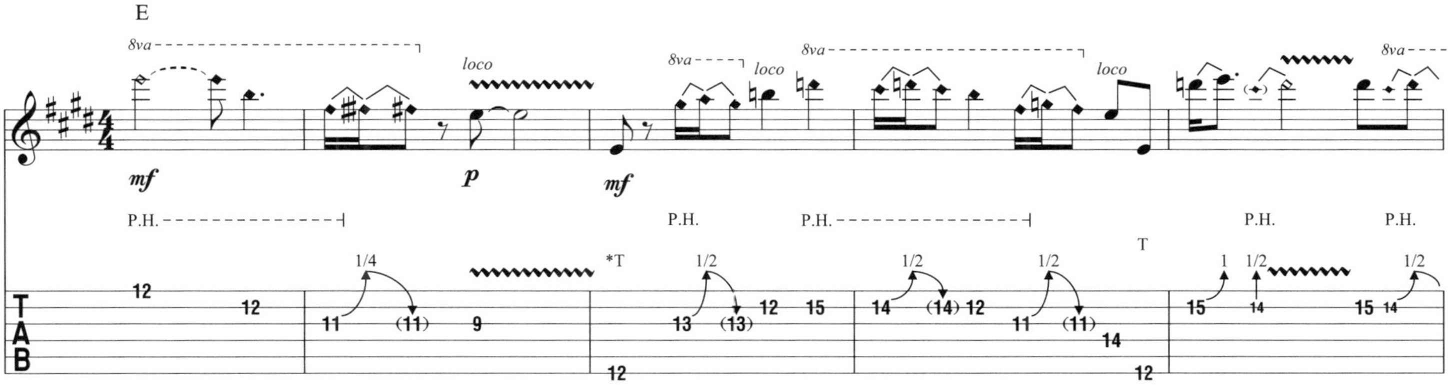

*T = Thumb on 6th string

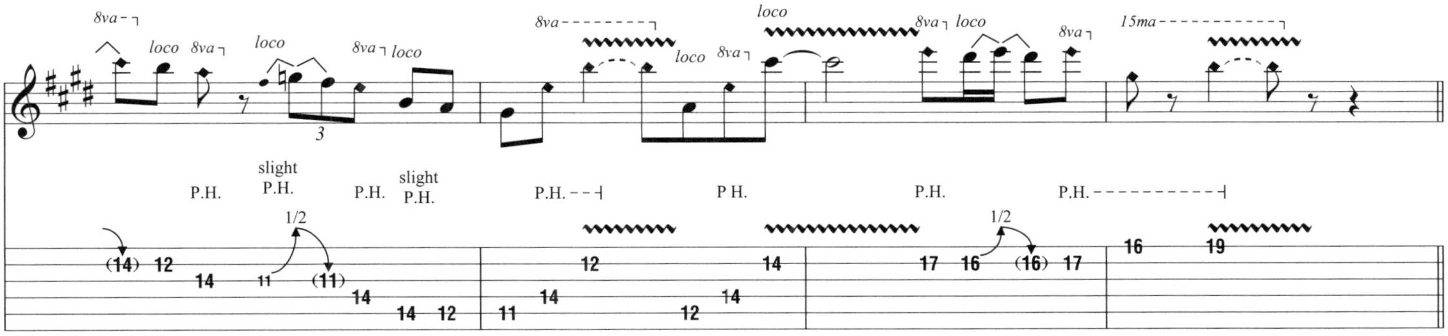

Example 90 (Fig. 36 on video): More ping harmonics
(0:45)

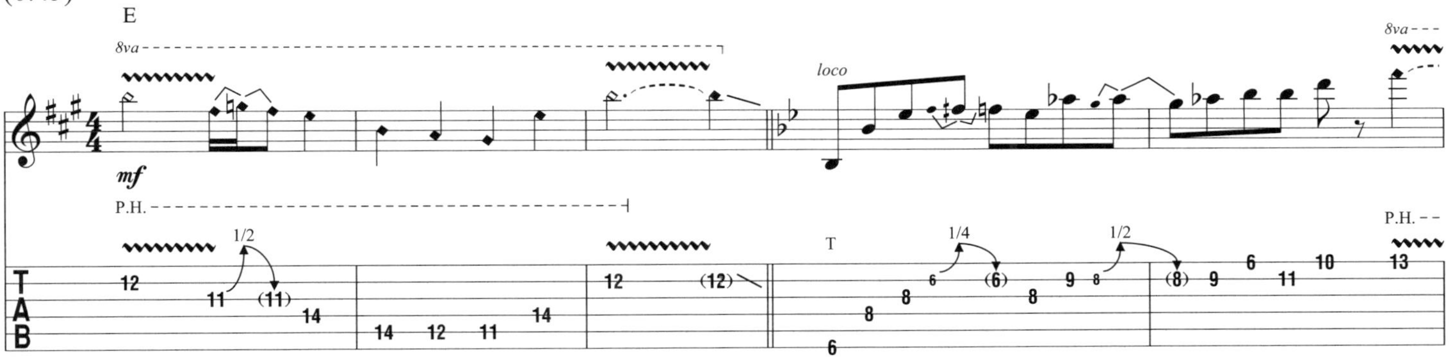

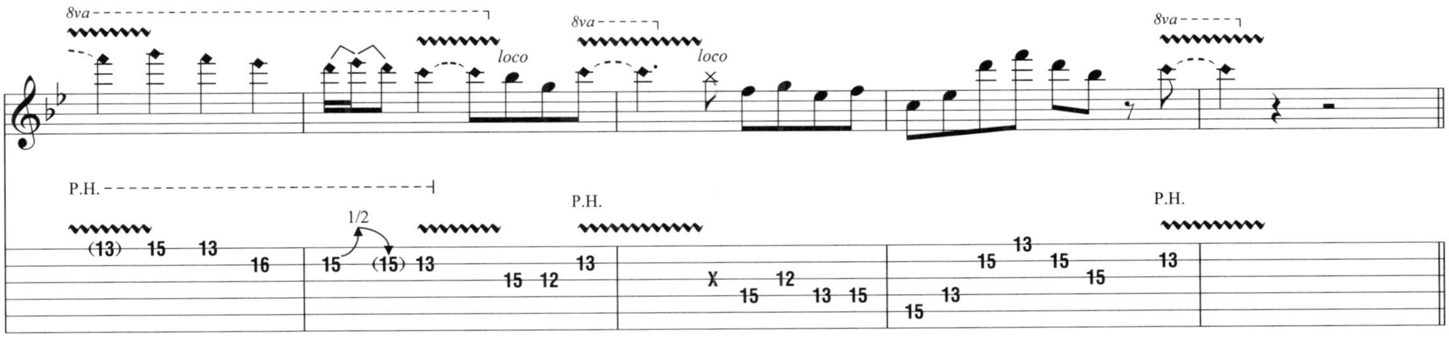

Example 91: Slap harmonics on chords, 12 frets above fretted note

(1:17)

*Artificial harmonics produced by slapping strings approx. 12 frets above fretted notes.

**Mute string w/ pick hand.

Example 92: Slap or "tap" harmonics 12 frets above the fretted notes
(1:53)

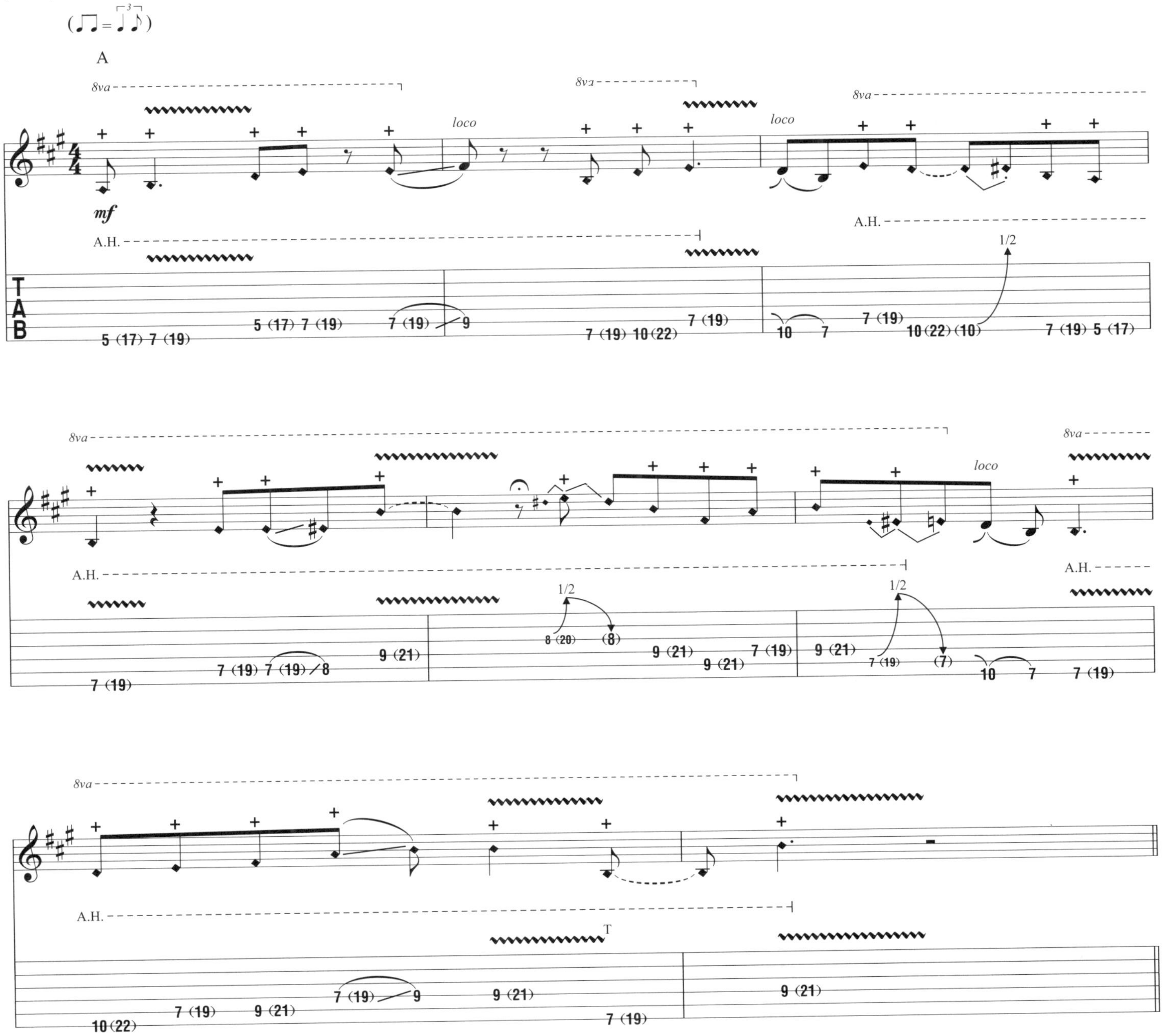

Example 93: Strummed chord harmonics
(2:21)

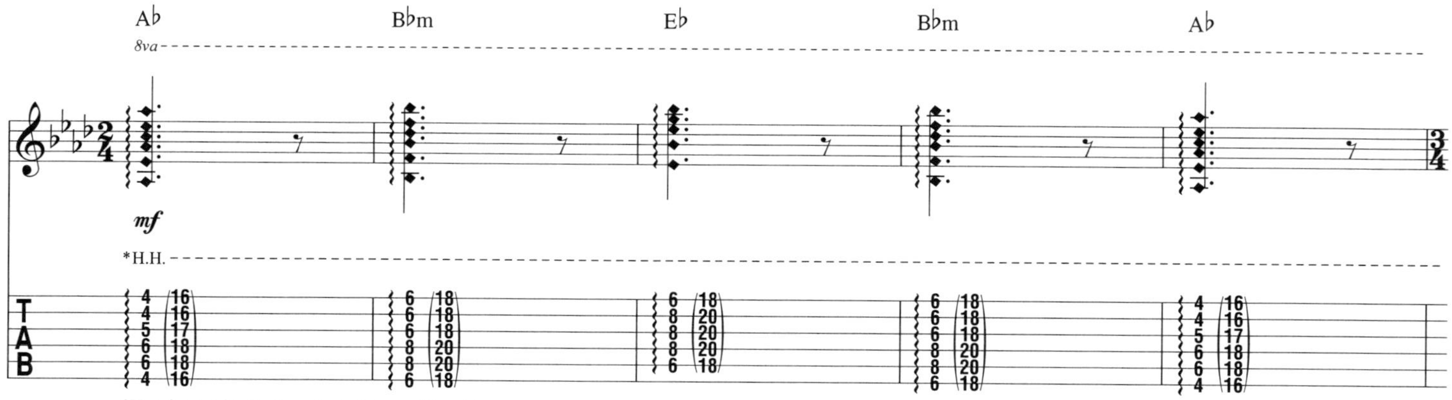

*Harp harmonics produced by lightly touching strings approx. 12 frets above fretted notes while picking string.

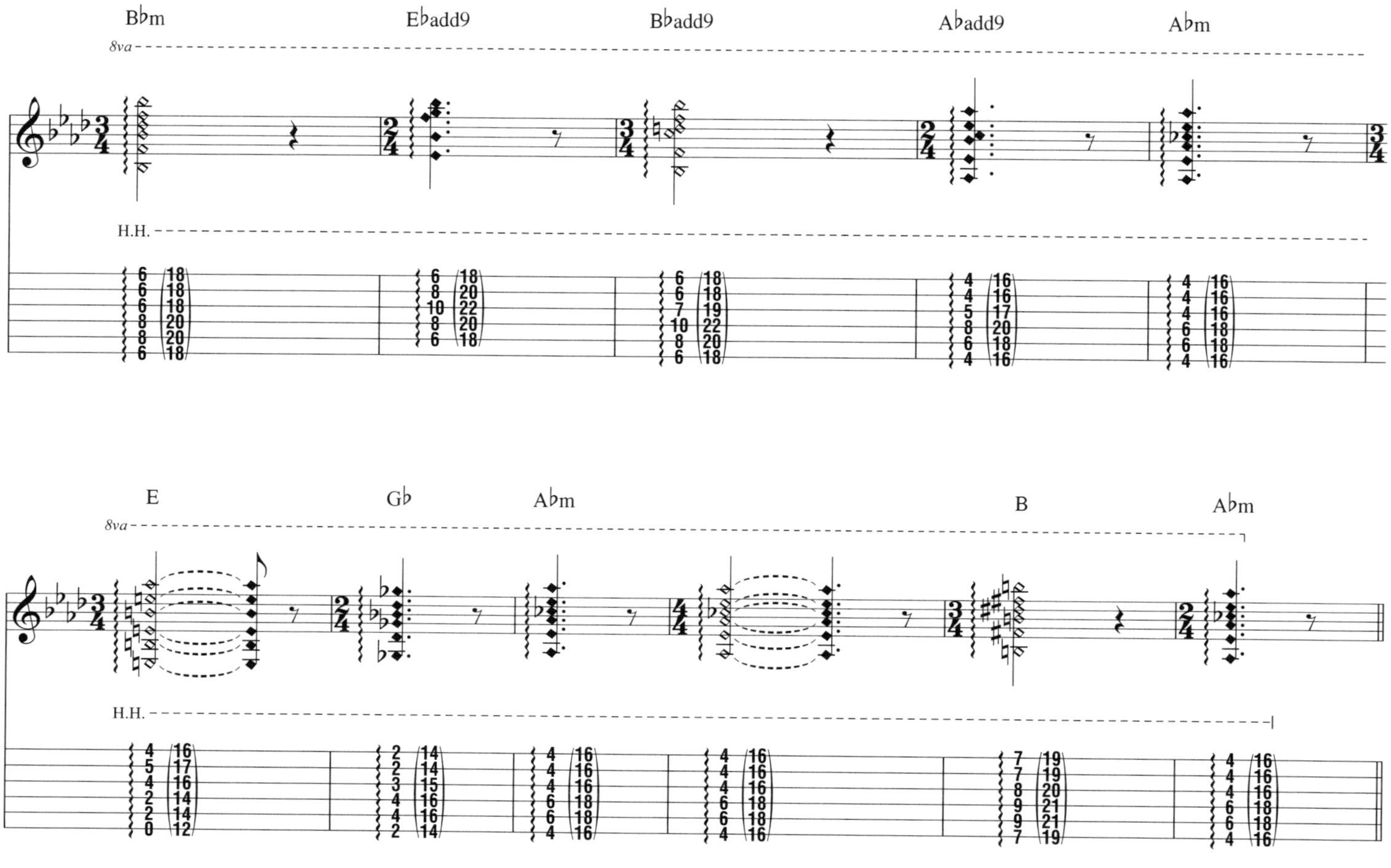

Example 94 (Fig. 37 on video): Artificial, or "classical," harmonics
(3:14)

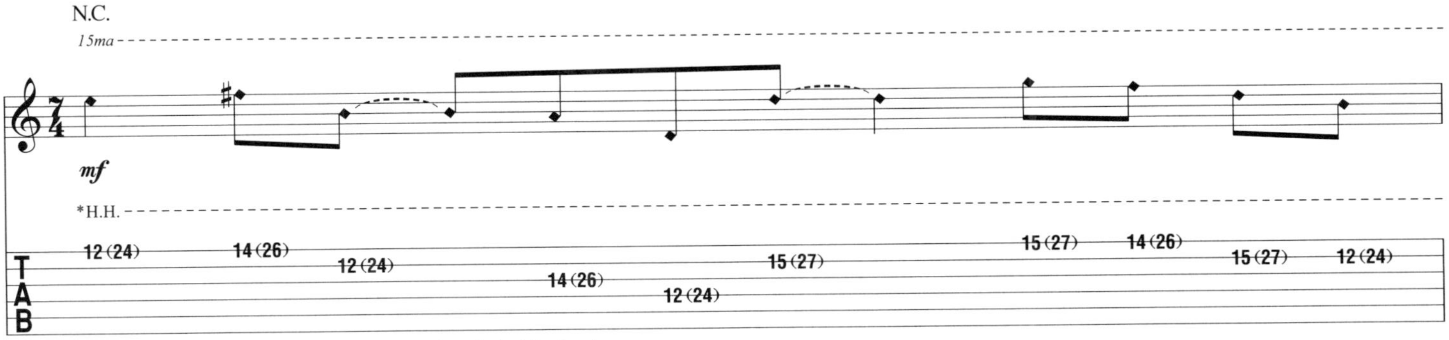

*Harp harmonics w/ pick. Notes in parenthesis are hypothetical fret locations.

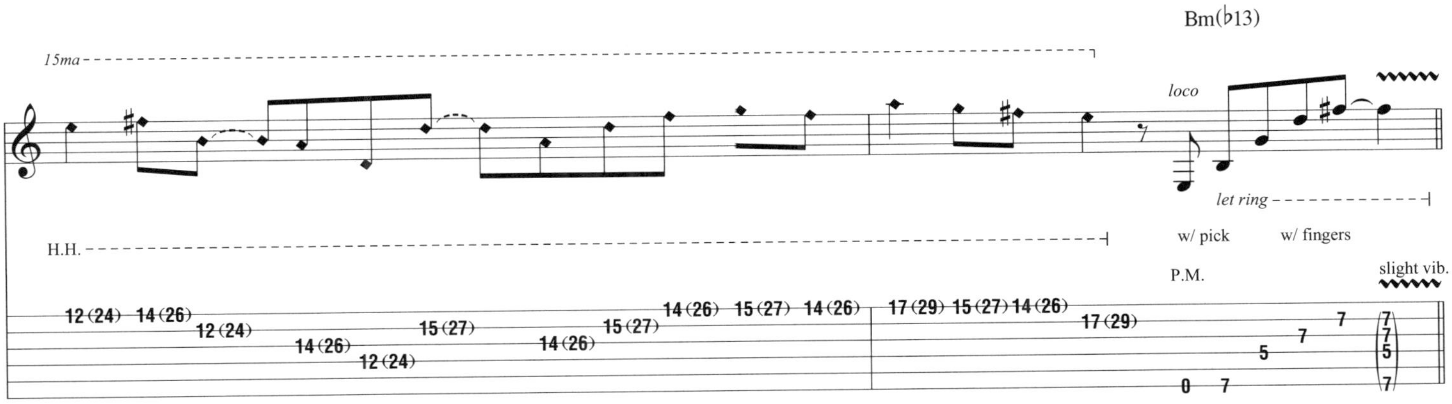

Example 95 (Fig. 38 on video): Lenny Breau style harp harmonics
(4:36)

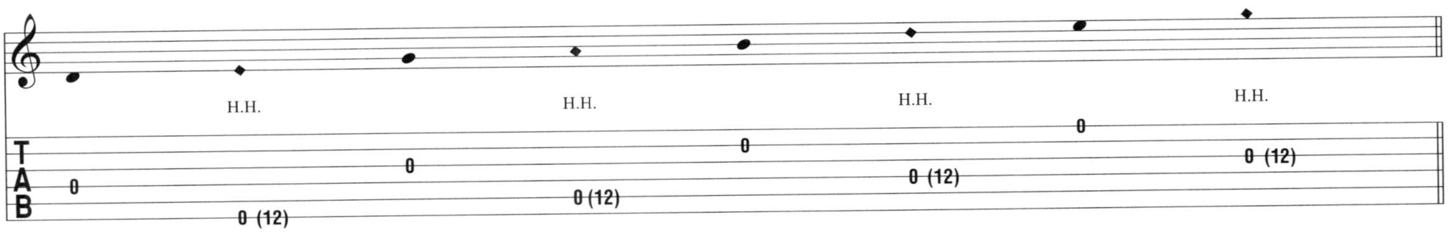

Example 96: Harp harmonics on chords
(4:54)

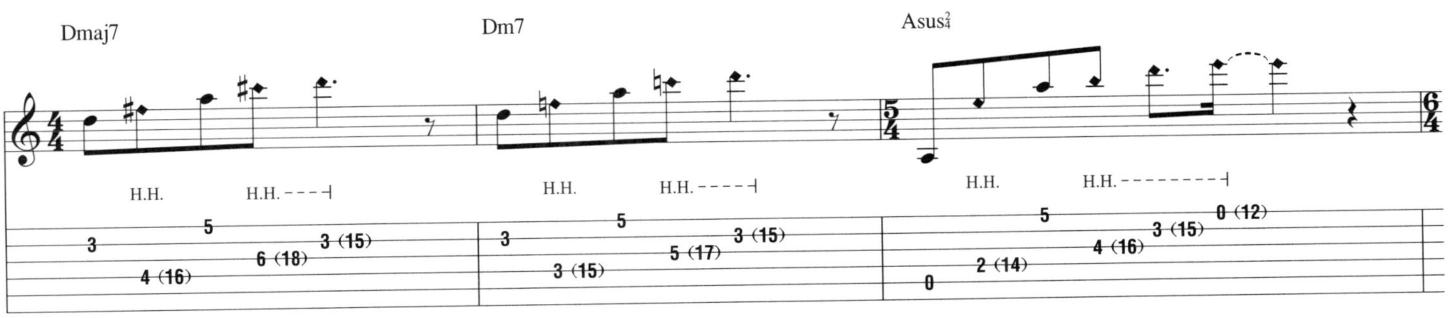

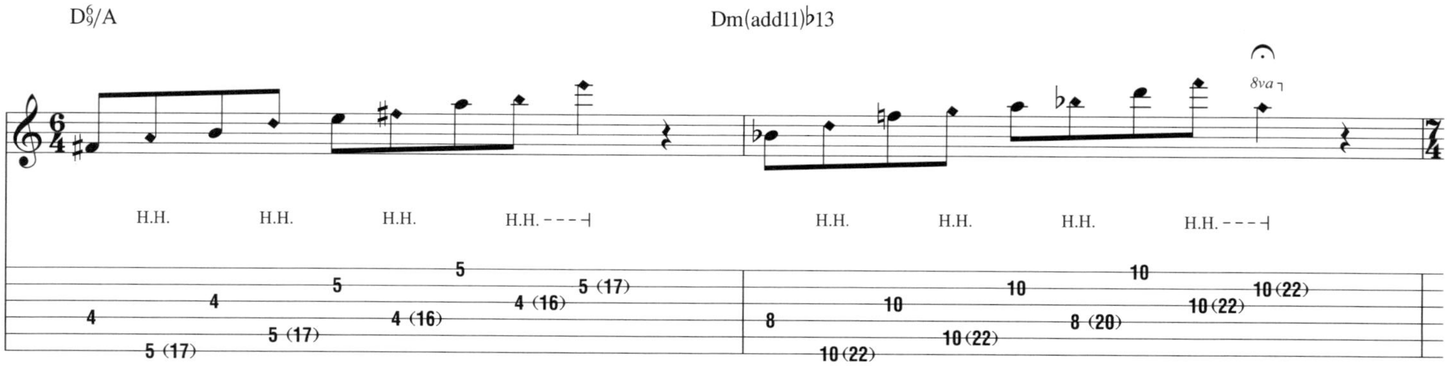

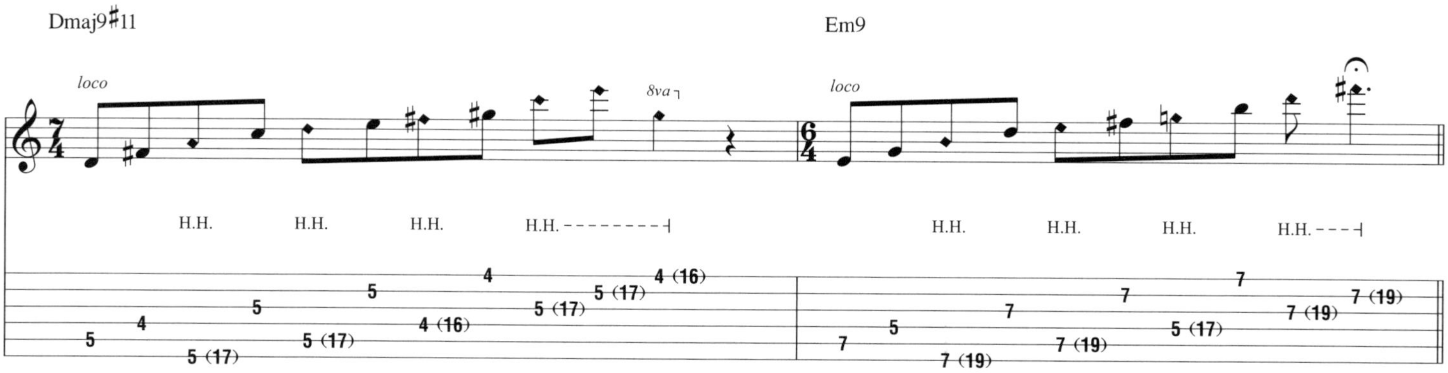

Example 97: Harp harmonics with pull-offs

(5:33)

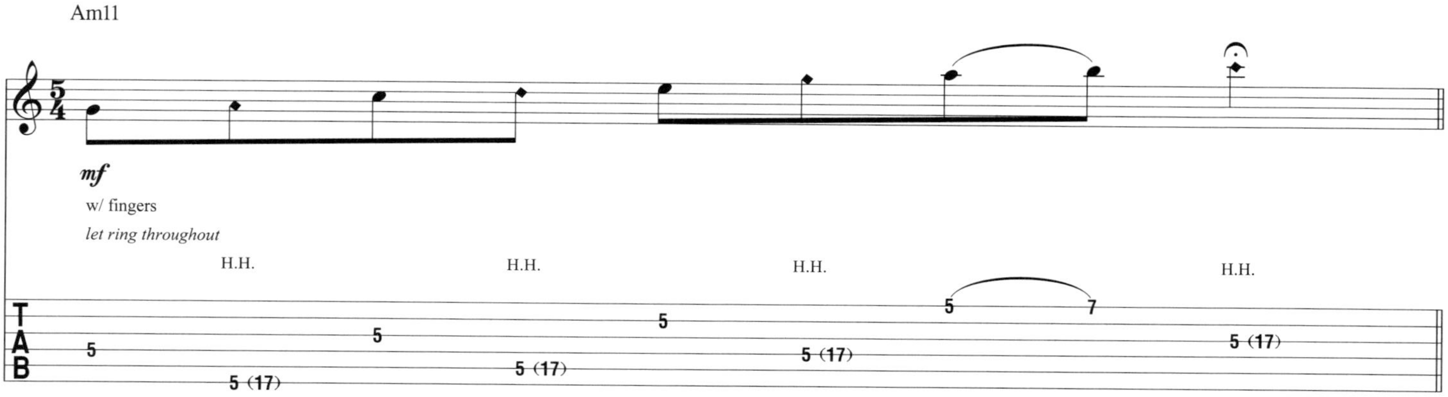

Example 98 (Fig. 39 on video): Harp harmonics in "cascading" fashion

(5:37)

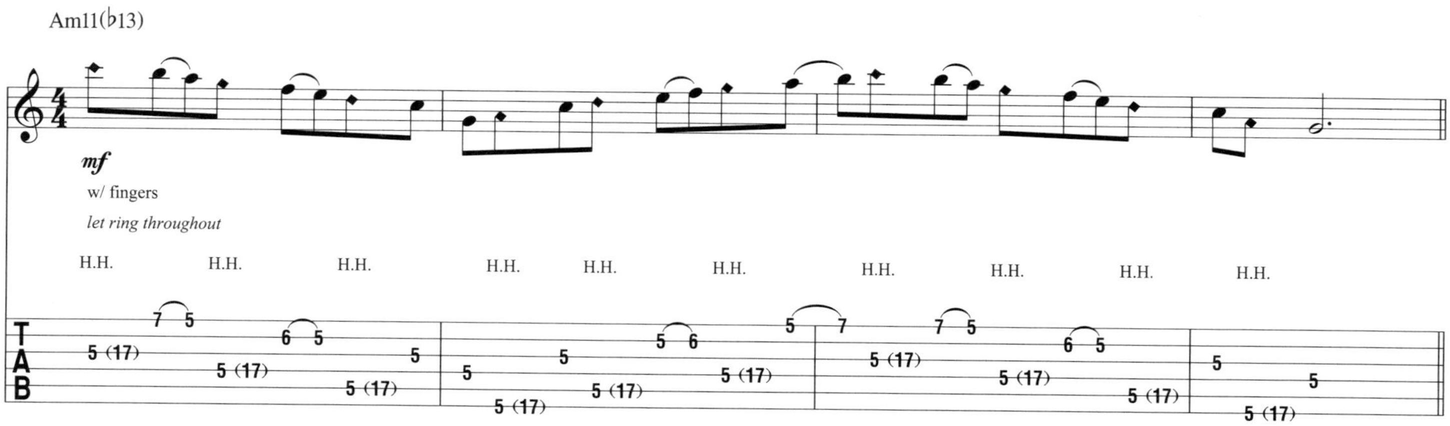

Example 99: Harmonics on dyads

(6:41)

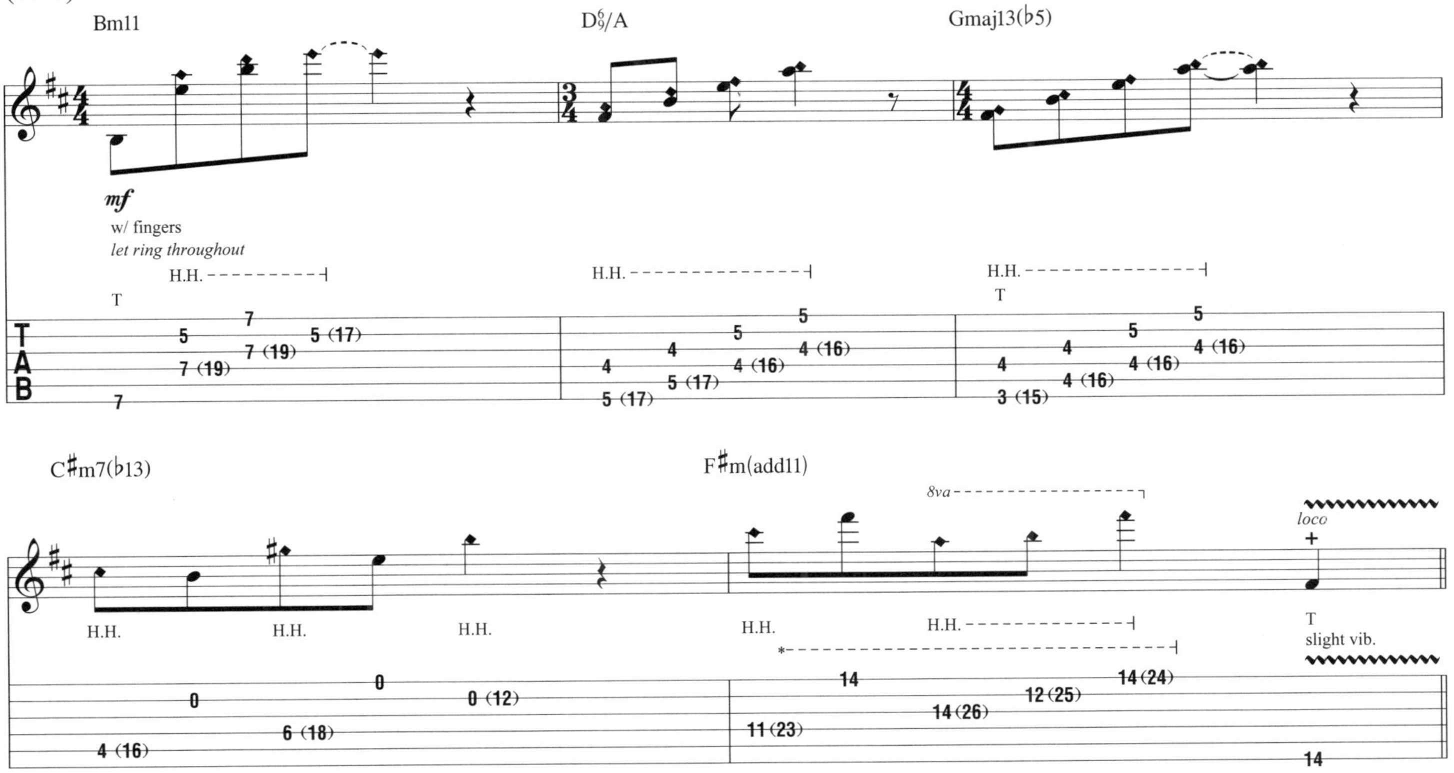

*Hypothetical fret locations.

Example 100: Integrating harmonics with chord passages

(7:15)

GUITAR NOTATION LEGEND

Guitar music can be notated three different ways: on a *musical staff*, in *tablature*, and in *rhythm slashes*.

RHYTHM SLASHES are written above the staff. Strum chords in the rhythm indicated. Use the chord diagrams found at the top of the first page of the transcription for the appropriate chord voicings. Round noteheads indicate single notes.

THE MUSICAL STAFF shows pitches and rhythms and is divided by bar lines into measures. Pitches are named after the first seven letters of the alphabet.

TABLATURE graphically represents the guitar fingerboard. Each horizontal line represents a string, and each number represents a fret.

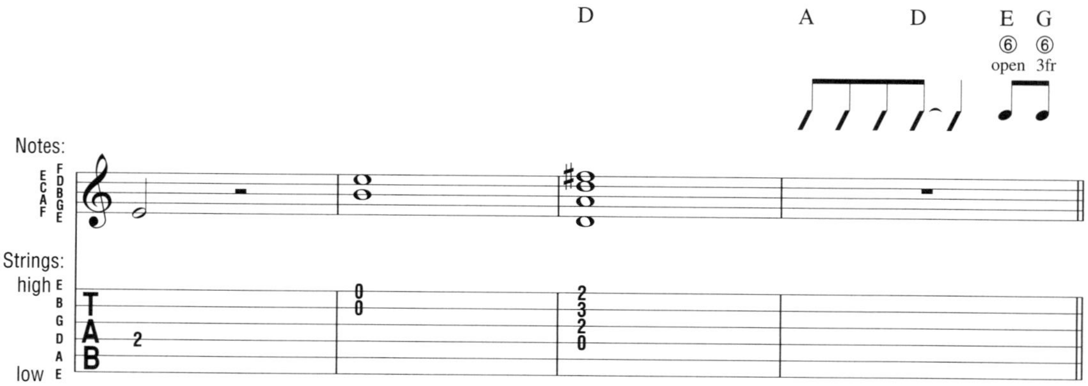

4th string, 2nd fret

1st & 2nd strings open, played together

open D chord

Definitions for Special Guitar Notation

HALF-STEP BEND: Strike the note and bend up 1/2 step.

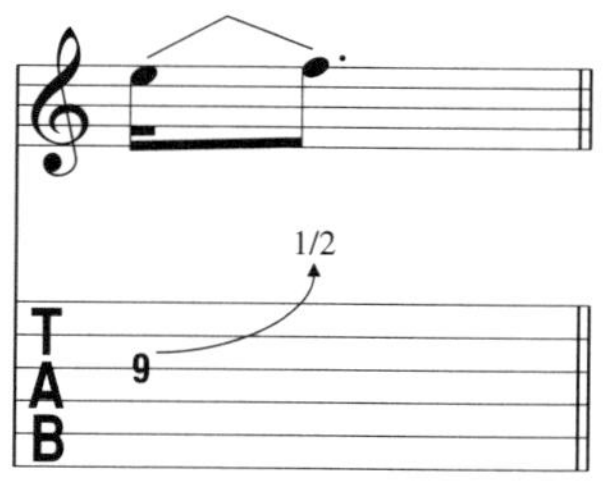

WHOLE-STEP BEND: Strike the note and bend up one step.

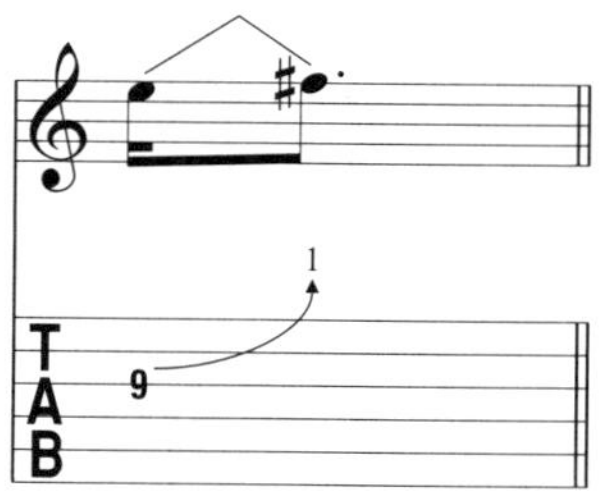

GRACE NOTE BEND: Strike the note and immediately bend up as indicated.

SLIGHT (MICROTONE) BEND: Strike the note and bend up 1/4 step.

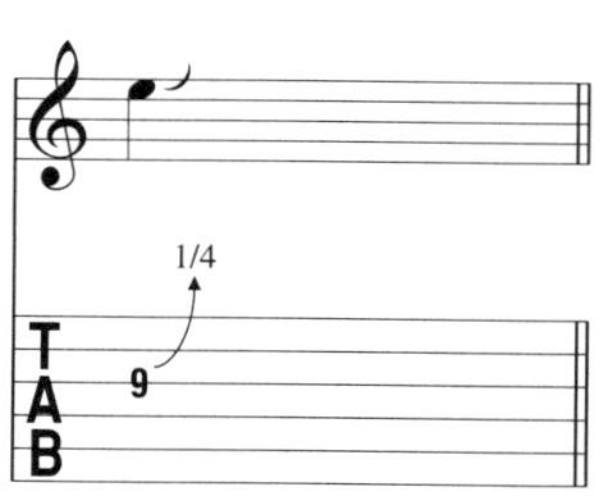

BEND AND RELEASE: Strike the note and bend up as indicated, then release back to the original note. Only the first note is struck.

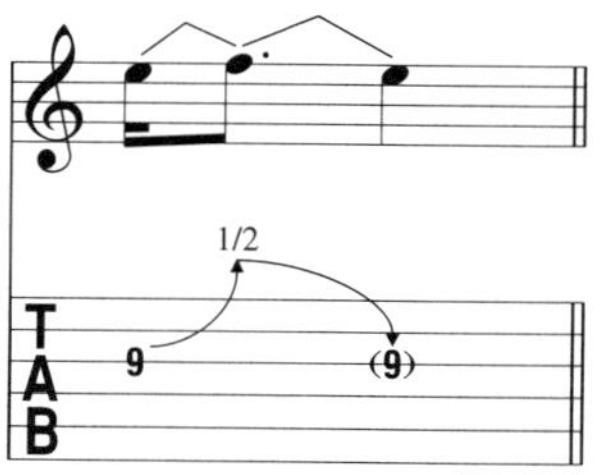

PRE-BEND: Bend the note as indicated, then strike it.

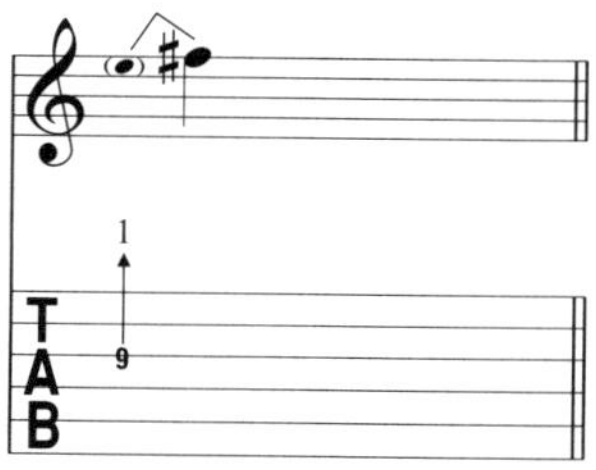

PRE-BEND AND RELEASE: Bend the note as indicated. Strike it and release the bend back to the original note.

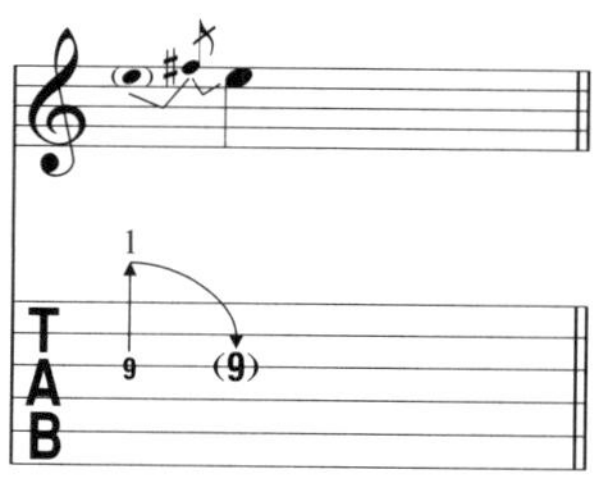

UNISON BEND: Strike the two notes simultaneously and bend the lower note up to the pitch of the higher.

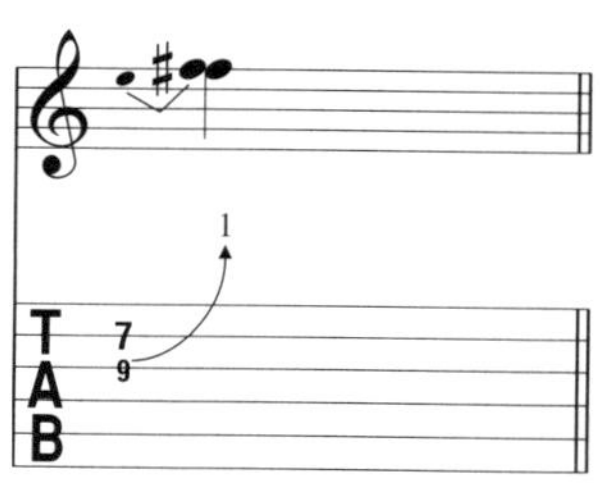

VIBRATO: The string is vibrated by rapidly bending and releasing the note with the fretting hand.

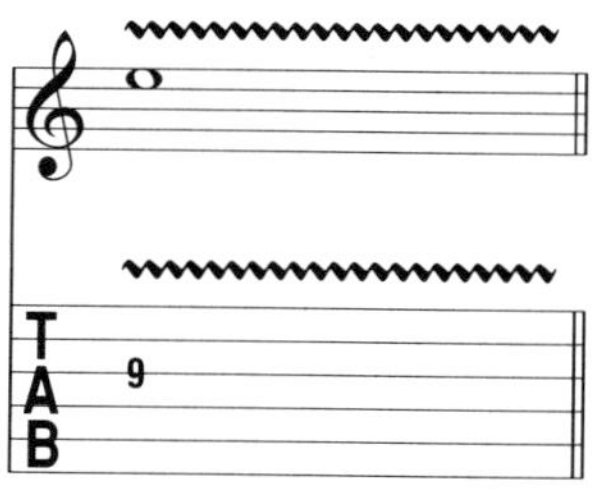

WIDE VIBRATO: The pitch is varied to a greater degree by vibrating with the fretting hand.

HAMMER-ON: Strike the first (lower) note with one finger, then sound the higher note (on the same string) with another finger by fretting it without picking.

PULL-OFF: Place both fingers on the notes to be sounded. Strike the first note and without picking, pull the finger off to sound the second (lower) note.

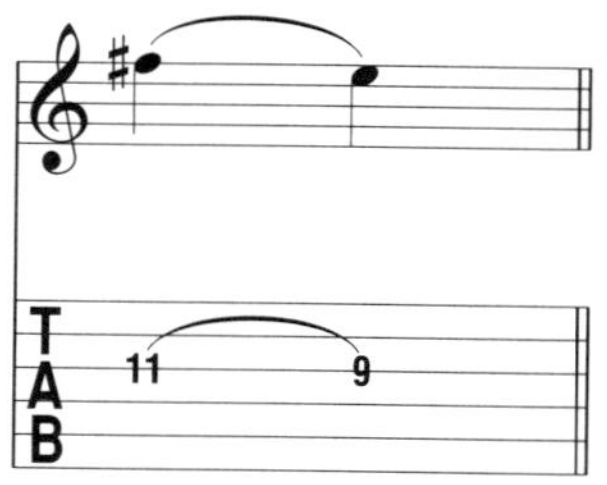

LEGATO SLIDE: Strike the first note and then slide the same fret-hand finger up or down to the second note. The second note is not struck.

SHIFT SLIDE: Same as legato slide, except the second note is struck.

TRILL: Very rapidly alternate between the notes indicated by continuously hammering on and pulling off.

TAPPING: Hammer ("tap") the fret indicated with the pick-hand index or middle finger and pull off to the note fretted by the fret hand.

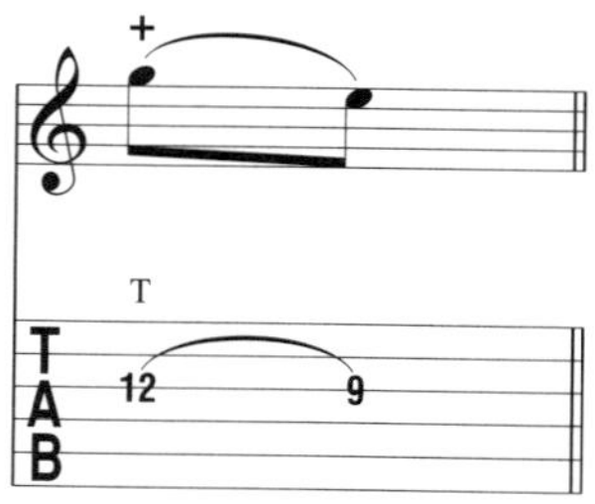

NATURAL HARMONIC: Strike the note while the fret-hand lightly touches the string directly over the fret indicated.

PINCH HARMONIC: The note is fretted normally and a harmonic is produced by adding the edge of the thumb or the tip of the index finger of the pick hand to the normal pick attack.

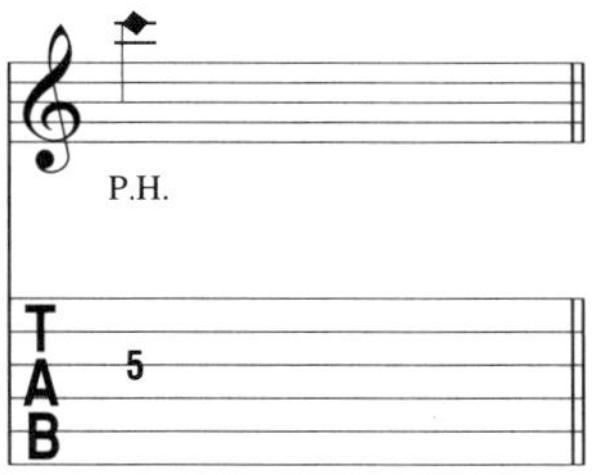

HARP HARMONIC: The note is fretted normally and a harmonic is produced by gently resting the pick hand's index finger directly above the indicated fret (in parentheses) while the pick hand's thumb or pick assists by plucking the appropriate string.

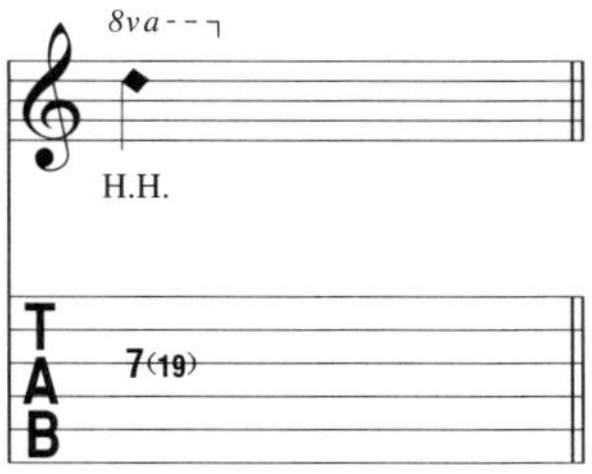

PICK SCRAPE: The edge of the pick is rubbed down (or up) the string, producing a scratchy sound.

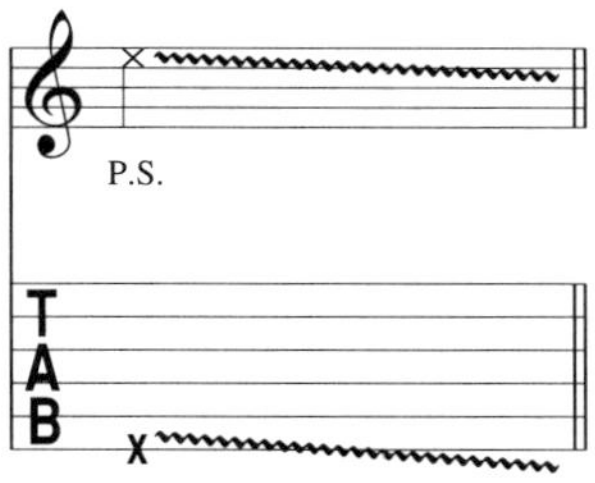

MUFFLED STRINGS: A percussive sound is produced by laying the fret hand across the string(s) without depressing, and striking them with the pick hand.

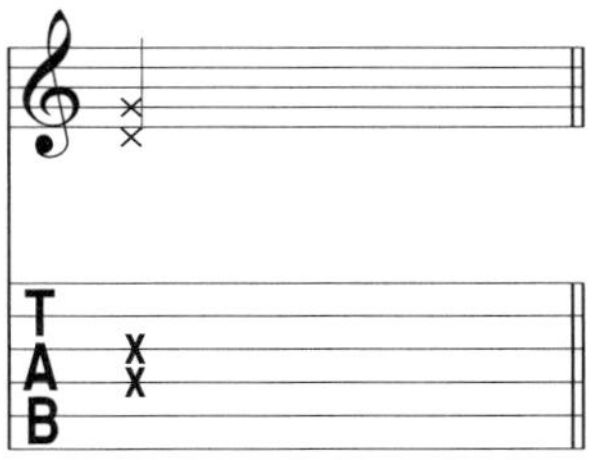

PALM MUTING: The note is partially muted by the pick hand lightly touching the string(s) just before the bridge.

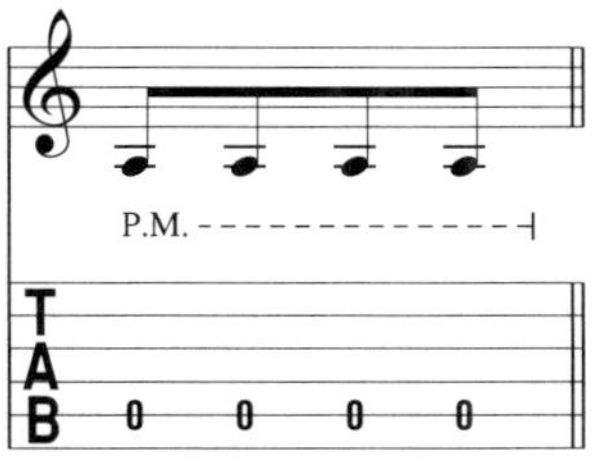

RAKE: Drag the pick across the strings indicated with a single motion.

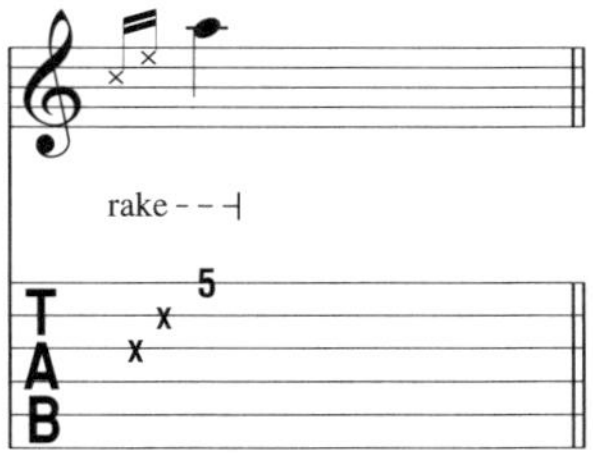

TREMOLO PICKING: The note is picked as rapidly and continuously as possible.

ARPEGGIATE: Play the notes of the chord indicated by quickly rolling them from bottom to top.

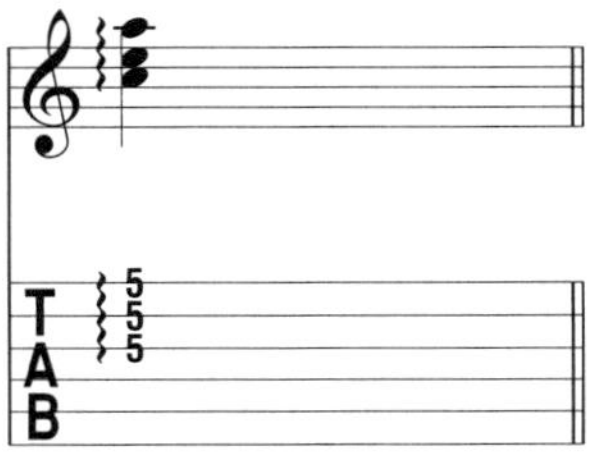

VIBRATO BAR DIVE AND RETURN: The pitch of the note or chord is dropped a specified number of steps (in rhythm), then returned to the original pitch.

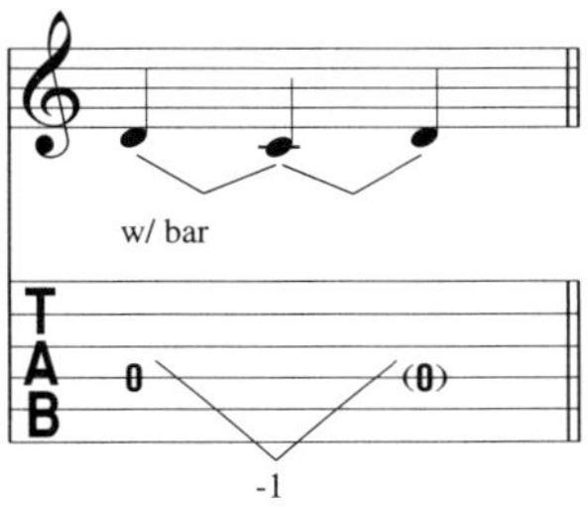

VIBRATO BAR SCOOP: Depress the bar just before striking the note, then quickly release the bar.

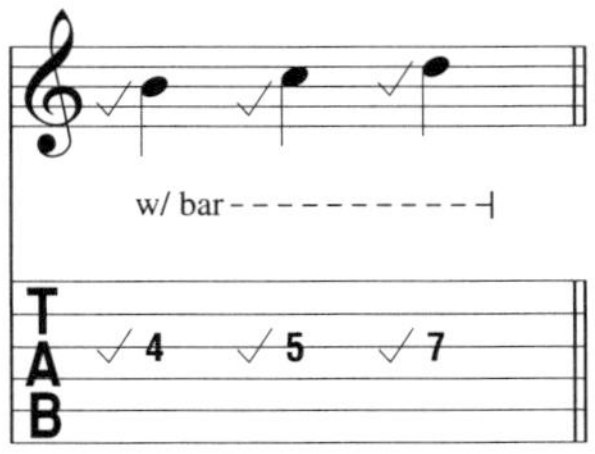

VIBRATO BAR DIP: Strike the note and then immediately drop a specified number of steps, then release back to the original pitch.

Additional Musical Definitions

 *(accent)* • Accentuate note (play it louder).

 *(accent)* • Accentuate note with great intensity.

 *(staccato)* • Play the note short.

⊓ • Downstroke

V • Upstroke

D.S. al Coda • Go back to the sign (𝄋), then play until the measure marked "***To Coda***," then skip to the section labelled "**Coda**."

D.C. al Fine • Go back to the beginning of the song and play until the measure marked "***Fine***" (end).

Rhy. Fig. • Label used to recall a recurring accompaniment pattern (usually chordal).

Riff • Label used to recall composed, melodic lines (usually single notes) which recur.

Fill • Label used to identify a brief melodic figure which is to be inserted into the arrangement.

Rhy. Fill • A chordal version of a Fill.

tacet • Instrument is silent (drops out).

 • Repeat measures between signs.

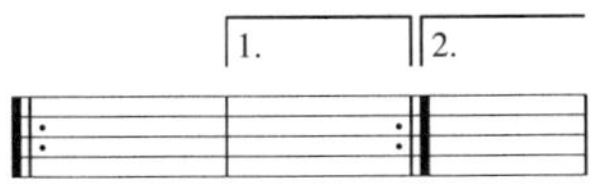

• When a repeated section has different endings, play the first ending only the first time and the second ending only the second time.

NOTE: Tablature numbers in parentheses mean:

1. The note is being sustained over a system (note in standard notation is tied), or
2. The note is sustained, but a new articulation (such as a hammer-on, pull-off, slide or vibrato) begins, or
3. The note is a barely audible "ghost" note (note in standard notation is also in parentheses).